CUBS
ESSENTIAL

Everything You Need to Know to Be a Real Fan!

Lew Freedman

TRIUMPH
BOOKS
CHICAGO

Library of Congress Cataloging-in-Publication Data

Freedman, Lew.
    Cubs essential : everything you need to know to be a real fan / Lew Freedman.
        p. cm.
    ISBN-13: 978-1-57243-816-3 (hard cover)
    ISBN-10: 1-57243-816-9 (hard cover)
        1. Chicago Cubs (Baseball team)—Miscellanea. 2. Chicago Cubs (Baseball team)—History.   I. Title

GV875.C6F74 2006
796.357'640977311—dc22

2005032421

This book is available in quantity at special discounts for your group or organization. For further information, contact:

Triumph Books
542 South Dearborn Street
Suite 750
Chicago, Illinois 60605
(312) 939-3330
Fax (312) 663-3557

Printed in U.S.A.
ISBN-13: 978-1-57243-816-3
ISBN-10: 1-57243-816-9
Design by Patricia Frey
Editorial production by Prologue Publishing Services
Photos courtesy of AP/Wide World Photos unless otherwise indicated.

To Ron Santo, Ernie Banks, Glenn Beckert, Don Kessinger, Ferguson Jenkins, Billy Williams, and Andy Pafko for the time they volunteered and for their insights.

Also to the long-suffering Chicago Cubs fans who have been waiting through the generations for a World Series championship since 1908. Your time is coming.

And to Cubs manager Dusty Baker, who had the courage and optimism to utter the phrase, "Why not us?"

Acknowledgments

First and foremost, the collection of files at the National Baseball Hall of Fame and Library in Cooperstown, New York, and the tremendous staff on site proved to be invaluable in helping me to research the Cubs back to the beginning of the franchise's existence.

Retired Cubs were generous in offering their insights about occurrences and experiences during their days with the club. Present-day ballplayers added a contemporary look to issues and games of import played more recently.

The clip files of Chicago newspapers, such as the *Tribune* and *Sun-Times,* provided accounts of key games, trades, and team developments from various seasons.

There is also a great body of baseball literature, especially on the Cubs, that was both fun to read and offered valuable help in pinpointing critical dates in the history of the team. First among equals when it comes to comprehensive information and a day-by-day reminder of just what happened and when is John Snyder's marvelous source, *Cubs Journal.*

Other notable Cubs-related books are *Holy Cow* by Harry Caray and Bob Verdi, *Few and Chosen* by Ron Santo and Phil Pepe, and *Touching Second* by Johnny Evers and Hugh Fullerton. Another source that is a wonderful memory prodder is the annual media guide put out by the Cubs team communications staff. The *2005 Cubs Information Guide* is the statistical bible of the team.

Introduction

The Cubs are as old as the National League. The franchise was born in 1876 as the Chicago White Stockings and is the only one that began then still continuously operating in the same city.

Some might argue that it is no coincidence that 1876 is the year of Custer's Last Stand. Foreshadowing. The leader of the Seventh Cavalry and his troops were being massacred on a Montana plain that summer, but the Cubs have had some fairly dismal Julys, too.

However, if the Cubs have been unable to shed a loveable loser's tag in recent decades—most likely because they are deeply loved and they have consistently been losers—it is worthwhile to note that once upon a time the team was the most dominant in the game.

Any team that has been in business for 130 years is bound to have some success, and the Cubs certainly did. It has, though, become trendy, if not somewhat repetitive, to dwell on the fact that the team has not been victorious in a World Series since 1908. Not very many people walking the planet during Teddy Roosevelt's presidency are around to recount the play-by-play. I do know a gentleman who is approaching 100 years of age, but he was a toddler at the time.

The Cubs of the famed double-play combination of Tinkers to Evers to Chance were a pre-1910 power. The Cubs of the 1930s, winning pennants on a three-year cycle, were one of the top clubs of that decade. But it has been 60 years since the Cubs last competed in a World Series, and around Chicago the sarcastic liken the rarity of such appearances to sightings of Halley's Comet.

The frustration grows among those who wish to observe a champion before going to meet their maker. Yet for those who grew up as loyal rooters, the habit is difficult to break. As the Cubs once again faded at mid-season in 2005, Chicago radio personality and confessed fan Marc Silverman correlated cheering for the Cubs to being afflicted with a disease.

"It's a slow death," he said. "A slow torture, and that's how they've done it for years and years."

Nonetheless, there is a richness to Cubs lore that compares favorably with that of any major league baseball team. The history is long, fascinating, often humorous, and periodically unbelievable. The fans who support the North Side club are as passionate as any in America and attend games at the rate of more than 3 million per season in one of the most storied pavilions in the land. Wrigley Field is regarded throughout the game as an architectural marvel and a monument to the sport's lyrical past and longevity.

In addition to contesting games in one of the grandest playgrounds in the land, Cubs lineage includes Tinkers, Evers, and Chance (immortalized in poetry); remarkable and aptly named Three Finger Brown; the stubby but powerful Hack Wilson; the extraordinary Mr. Cub, Ernie Banks; the beloved team of 1969; the colorful ambassador of the game, Harry Caray; and everything from the bizarre soap opera finish of the 2003 season to the Curse of the Billy Goat.

For well more than a century, the Cubs have teased and entertained their fans, and if the rewards have sometimes seemed minimal, they have certainly always provided fodder for never-ending conversation.

Simply attending a Cubs game may require an interpreter. Emblazoned upon a Sheffield Avenue apartment building behind the right-field wall are the words, "Eamus Catuli."

No, that is not the name of a revered retired outfielder from the 1920s. The words are Latin for "Let's Go Cubs!"

The theme and sentiment endure.

Beginnings

Tinker to Evers to Chance was once as famous an American threesome as Moe, Larry, and Curly.

Which was ironic. Shortstop Joe Tinker and second baseman Johnny Evers hated each other. Frank Chance was their first baseman and manager, and tolerated their feud as long as they scooped up grounders and made accurate throws.

Chance was irritated by the constant carping at umpires in which the diminutive Evers engaged, and once said he wished Evers played the outfield so he couldn't hear his unceasing negative chatter. It was not by accident Evers was nicknamed "the Crab."

The renown of the Cubs double-play combination owed less to skill than to the creative pen of Franklin P. Adams, who published a little ditty in the *New York Evening Mail* on July 18, 1910, titled "Baseball's Sad Lexicon":

These are the saddest of possible words:
"Tinker to Evers to Chance."
Trio of bear cubs, and fleeter than birds.
Tinker and Evers and Chance,
Ruthlessly pricking our gonfalon bubble,
Making a Giant hit into a double—
Words that are heavy with nothing but trouble:
"Tinker to Evers to Chance."

Proving that it never hurts to have a good press agent, all three were later elected to the Baseball Hall of Fame—and they did not even constitute the Cubs' best infield of all time (think 1960s). It helped simply that

Tinker was one-third of the Tinker-to-Evers-to-Chance Cubs double-play combination made famous in poetic terms that helped usher the trio into the Baseball Hall of Fame.

Tinker, Evers, and Chance were efficient when the double play was first popularized in the box score on September 15, 1902. In a way, it gave them the same sort of cachet more recently reserved for basketball players who accomplish a triple double.

TRIVIA

Who is the pitcher who threw the first no-hitter in Cubs history?

Answers to the trivia questions are on pages 158–159.

The gang could pull off a double play together, but don't try to seat them at the same dinner table. Their icy interpersonal relationships eliminated off-field socializing. Sometimes it seemed they actually behaved like the Three Stooges. Tinker placed the origin of bad feelings at 1908 or 1909. One day, he said, the team was playing an exhibition game in Bedford, Indiana. The habit was to dress at the hotel, then share rides in horse-drawn taxis to the park. Evers took off by himself, leaving a steaming Tinker and impatient teammates with a long wait for the next ride.

"I was mad, and when I got to the park we got into a fight," Tinker recalled.

Evers, who wrote an autobiography called *Touching Second* with sportswriter Hugh Fullerton (whose efforts helped expose the Black Sox Scandal), once said that he and Tinker spoke only in anger after 1908.

And they were teammates through the 1912 season.

"Every time something went wrong on the field, we would be at each other and there would be a fight in the clubhouse after the game," he said. "Joe weighed 175 pounds and I weighed about 135, but that didn't make any difference to either of us. He'd rush at me and get me by the throat and I'd punch him in the belly and try to cut him with my spikes, and then Chance or one of the other big guys would come to my rescue."

Decades later, Tinker and Evers were coincidentally scheduled to appear on the same sports broadcast, made peace, and became friends. Evers had apparently mellowed somewhat in older age and reflected on his relationship with Chance, too.

"It's a wonder Chance didn't kill me," Evers said. "Nobody could talk to him like I could, and I would make him madder than anybody."

Well after he retired, Evers met Adams for the first time and, paying homage to the power of the press, said, "I owe you a lasting debt of gratitude for keeping my name before the public all these years. I'd've been

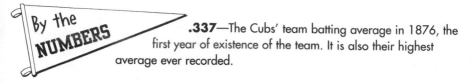

By the NUMBERS

.337—The Cubs' team batting average in 1876, the first year of existence of the team. It is also their highest average ever recorded.

forgotten long ago if it wasn't for 'Baseball's Sad Lexicon.'" Evers died at the age of 65 in 1947, and Tinker died on his 68th birthday in 1948.

If any of the threesome deserved special acknowledgment, it was probably Chance. Known as "the Peerless Leader," Chance batted .297 in 16 years of play and managed the Cubs to four pennants and two World Series championships. A manager who compiled such a leadership record today in Chicago would have a statue erected of him in the Loop.

The magnificent manager John McGraw called Chance not only a great first baseman, but a notable leader "because he asked no man to take any chance that he would not take himself, and because he had the power to instill enthusiasm even in a losing cause."

Compared to the losing causes that were to come, that era's losing was an eyeblink in the passage of seasons.

Chance did not accept defeat calmly. Once, after the Cubs lost to the Giants by one run while leaving 12 men on base, he was said to be grumpy at home, refusing to eat dinner and brooding in the living room.

His wife reportedly tried to soothe Chance, stroking his hair and saying, "Don't worry, dear, you still have me."

"Maybe so," Chance replied, "but there was many a time this afternoon when I'd have traded you for a base hit."

By the time Tinker, Evers, and Chance gained notoriety, the Chicago franchise was an institution among "western" clubs. The National League was founded February 2, 1876, in New York, and Chicago was represented, winning the first league title. Chicago championships followed in 1880, 1881, 1882, 1885, and 1886.

In its earliest days, the Chicago team had about the same number of nicknames as the Lincoln Park Zoo has animals. Before adopting the name "Cubs" in 1902, the organization was known as the Colts, Black Stockings, Ex-Colts, Rainmakers, Orphans, Cowboys, Rough Riders, Remnants, Recruits, Panamas, Zephyrs, Nationals, Spuds, and Trojans. For a brief period they were called the Microbes. Perhaps the imaginations of all in the Windy City were exhausted after 28 years of being put under a microscope and shuffling the brand name, but "Cubs" stuck

Chance, known as the "Peerless Leader" during his playing and managing days, once rebuffed his wife's attempts to soothe him after a tough loss by informing her he would have traded her for a base hit that afternoon.

after the *Chicago Daily American* advanced the suggestion in its editions of March 27, 1902. Chance, for one, supported the choice.

Albert Spalding, who founded the sporting goods empire that bore his name, managed the first two Chicago teams. But soon began the Adrian "Cap" Anson era. Anson, who compiled a .327 lifetime batting average in 22 seasons, and served as manager nearly as long, is clearly one of the most outstanding players in Cubs history.

Not his usual double-play partner. Johnny Evers frolics with Giants manager John McGraw's dog—perhaps filling in as a fourth member of the renowned infield?

IF ONLY ... Cubs revered player and skipper Frank Chance had been more careful in the batter's box. A bold hitter, Chance sacrificed his body too many times. Numerous beanings forced him into retirement with severe headaches in 1914, and he died prematurely at age 47 in September 1924.

However, his reprehensible behavior on more than one occasion toward black players on other teams would have led to his ruination in more modern, enlightened times. Anson refused to allow his Chicago club to take the field for an exhibition game against a squad from Newark because it fielded a black player. Later, in April 1883, Anson tried to bully the Toledo team into benching Moses Fleetwood Walker and his brother Weldy Walker against Chicago because they were black. Toledo refused, and the game went on. Later that year, however, Anson faced down a Toledo team then in financial straits, and the Walkers sat out an exhibition.

Anson, who was born in 1852 in Marshalltown, Iowa, wrote an autobiography in 1900 called *A Ball Player's Career*. In it he occasionally ridicules black speech in dialect.

From the standpoint of both history and storytelling, the Chicagos (as they were also sometimes called) made a mark in their first three decades of play. Billy Sunday played for the team between 1883 (two years after the gunfight at the OK Corral in Tombstone) and 1887 before discovering his calling. Sunday became a nationally famous religious figure—who began preaching against Sunday baseball. Perhaps he was merely possessive of his name.

Of Sunday, Anson wrote, he "was as good a boy who ever lived, being conscientious in a marked degree, hardworking, good-natured, and obliging.

"Since Bill retired from the diamond he has become noted as an evangelist and I am told by those who should know that he is a brilliant speaker and a great success in that line."

John Clarkson, who won 329 games and became a Hall of Famer in 1963, was the Chicagos' first great pitcher. In 1885 his record was 53–16 over 623 innings. They didn't know from closers back then. The only relief offered was a bucket of ice when the game ended. A year later,

Clarkson struck out 16 men in a game, a team record until 1998, when Kerry Wood struck out 20.

During those days, ballplayers arrived at the park in style in horse-drawn carriages, that era's equivalent of 300-horsepower sports cars.

The most amazing road trip of the early years of the franchise was a goodwill adventure taken in late 1888 and early 1889. After crossing oceans by ship, the Chicagos played a 28-game series of exhibitions against the All-America All-Stars in Egypt, in the shadow of the pyramids. Anson wrote of playing games in Ceylon, Italy, France, and England, where there were showdowns with cricket players. In the course of doing their duty for American foreign policy, the players met President Benjamin Harrison, who thought the whole thing was a neat enterprise.

Just to illustrate that baseball players have indulged in unusual side behavior from the dawn of the game, in 1894 Chicago catcher Pop Schriver caught a ball dropped 500 feet from the observation deck of the Washington Monument. At the time the structure was only nine years old and still sparkled with its freshness.

Upon the monument's construction, players became intrigued by the idea of whether such a catch could be made with the receiver avoiding death or serious injury. A handful of players attempted to make such a catch, but didn't pull it off. At least no one got conked. On August 25—somewhat remarkably with the encouragement of manager Anson—several players trooped to the monument, and a group climbed to the observation deck. A ball was dropped, but Schriver, gauging the velocity, let it hit the ground and bounce. When it did not ricochet as high as he feared, he settled under the second ball heaved over the deck's side and made the grab. In modern times, no doubt, the players on the deck and Schriver himself would be arrested, liability issues would be raised, and the club would fear for its investment.

On May 5, 1890, during a lull in the winning ways of the team, the Cubs entertained just 125 people in the West Side Grounds stadium during a 2–2 tie with the Reds, called because of darkness. Just to show that Schriver had no monopoly on player wackiness, in an April 1902 game, a rookie pitcher named Jim St. Vrain hit a grounder to Pirates shortstop Honus Wagner and befuddled all witnesses by running to third base.

Cap Anson plays a signficant role in Cubs history, both as an accomplished player and long-time manager. However, his tenure was marred by his racist attitudes.

By the time the Cubs' name began to take hold and the infield of Tinker, Evers, and Chance (Harry Steinfeldt was the less-famously recalled third baseman) in 1902, Chicago was on the cusp of a fresh dynasty.

The Cubs made their debut in the then-fledgling World Series in 1906. The team set a record with its 116–36 regular-season mark and was a heavy favorite to crush "the Hitless Wonder" White Sox, who batted only .230 and struck just seven home runs. In the only all-Chicago World Series, the White Sox pulled off a four-games-to-two upset. Cubs fans are still upset, too.

Despite the stunner, the World Series appearance was the start of a flush period for the Cubs. In 1907 Chicago returned to the series and swept the Detroit Tigers. It was the Cubs' first World Series championship. In 1908 the Cubs met the Tigers again and triumphed four games

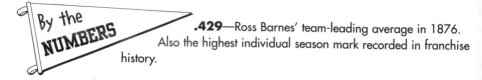

.429—Ross Barnes' team-leading average in 1876. Also the highest individual season mark recorded in franchise history.

to one. It was their last world championship. In 1910 the Cubs landed in their fourth World Series in five seasons, losing to the Philadelphia A's.

Near the end of the 1908 regular season, the Cubs were participants in one of the most infamous plays in major league history. The game pitted the Cubs against the New York Giants at the Polo Grounds on September 23. As a three-way pennant race between the two clubs and the Pirates culminated, the Cubs and Giants were tied 1–1 with two outs in the last of the ninth inning.

New York had runners on first and third. A single by Al Bridwell scored the base runner from third. Frank Merkle was on first and thought the game was over. Instead of running to second base, he began working his way to the clubhouse. The celebrating crowd ran to the field as Cubs players, misplaying the ball in Keystone Cops fashion, frantically sought to get the ball to Evers. Evers actually wrenched the ball away from a fan and stepped on second. Umpire Hank O'Day called Merkle out.

Citing darkness and the crowd stampeding over the field, O'Day ruled the game a tie, and the league office backed him up, calling for a replay of the game. The Pirates were eliminated, the Cubs won the playoff to advance to the World Series, and the angry Giants went home. The mistake has been forever known as "Merkle's Boner."

It was the type of ruling in later years that pessimistic Cubs fans felt would go against them.

"We players finally got through the crowd to the clubhouse, dressed, and went downtown," said Tinker. "It wasn't until that night that we found out O'Day had called Merkle out and declared the game a 1–1 tie."

The stalwart pitcher of the successful early 20th century Cubs teams was Mordecai Centennial Brown, who was bestowed the middle name because he was born in Indiana on the 100th anniversary of the U.S.A. When Brown was seven years old, he caught his right hand in a corn-grinding machine on the farm, and it clipped off two fingers. Another accident further damaged Brown's hand, but when it came to baseball he was known to throw what was described as "a hellacious curveball."

Brown later said, "All I knew is that I had all the fingers I needed." He was right. Brown won 239 games and recorded a 2.06 earned-run average. He was paid $10,000 in 1913 to write seven lessons' worth of

*entury after he
ew for the Cubs,
rdecai "Three
ger" Brown
nains one of the
atest pitchers in
nchise history.
wn was victimized
a farm accident as
hild—hence the
kname—but was
le to master a
vastating curveball.*

pitching instruction. In the advertising, Brown is called "the world's champion professional pitcher," and it goes on to say he has "put down in writing the whole truth about pitching. Nothing is held back—he tells you everything." In part one, Brown disparages luck and emphasizes "pluck," something he surely epitomized.

When Brown died at 71 in 1948, people in his hometown of Terre Haute built a statue in his honor.

Despite featuring some of the most accomplished Cubs players in the history of the franchise, a century later even the most casual of team fans most clearly recalls one number—1908. That is the last year the Chicago Cubs won a World Series.

Wrigley Field Is Born

It cost $250,000 to build Wrigley Field in 1914. The minimum salary for a major league player during the 2005 season was $316,000. Never mind that in 2005 America obtaining a three-bedroom house in a pleasant neighborhood for a quarter-million dollars involved major league sleuthing.

Under their various nicknames, the Cubs had long played at the West Side Grounds, but like many ballparks of the day, it was primarily made of wood and subject to destruction by fire. Although the Wrigley family, the chewing gum magnates, long have been associated with the Friendly Confines and its gradual development into the park we all know today, it was prior owner Charles H. Weeghman who ordered construction. Weeghman operated the Chicago Whales of the briefly vibrant alternative circuit, the Federal League.

Ground for the new steel-and-concrete structure was broken March 1, 1914, and in a miracle of the sort unknown to current-day construction, the park located at the corner of Addison and Clark on the North Side was finished in seven weeks. It was the Whales, defeating Kansas City 9–1 on April 23, who christened the park. After the 1915 season, however, the Federal League went belly up, and the Cubs moved in.

The Cubs' Weeghman Park debut took place April 20, 1916, and the hosts won 7–6 over the Reds in 11 innings. Some 18,000 fans attended. To mark the occasion, a bear cub shipped from Alaska was presented by fans to club president Charles Thomas. For some time, the cub, named Joa, lived in a cage on Addison Street. Weeghman, a wealthy restaurant owner, put together a syndicate to buy the Cubs. His team included William Wrigley Jr., who ultimately bought the controlling interest and

By the
NUMBERS

2—The number of seasons all-time great Frank Chance led the club in home runs. In 1904 Chance's team-leading total was six. In 1905 Chance tied for the team lead with two other players. All hit just two homers.

by 1927 had changed the name of the park to Wrigley Field, which had been known as Cubs Park for a brief stretch.

Wrigley was state-of-the-art when new, but over time, as all other early 20th-century parks crumbled and were replaced (except for Fenway Park in Boston), it became an icon of the game, a symbol of the timelessness of baseball crossing generations. Chicago fans came to see the stadium—expanded and renovated many times in many ways over the years—as a shrine as much as a ballpark. Fans across the land made pilgrimages to Chicago just so they could say they once watched a game in Wrigley Field.

"Wrigley Field stayed the way it was," said Glenn Beckert, the Cubs' All-Star second baseman of the 1960s who now lives in Florida. "I played in the period when they were building these new, colossal stadiums, where everything was the same distance in right field, left field. Now some of the new ballparks are going back to the Wrigley design. They're smaller parks."

Not merely home to a baseball team, Wrigley is a Lakeview neighborhood fixture. It was built at a time when Americans did not rely on the automobile, and apartment buildings, restaurants, saloons, and shops expanded and took over the area that would become known as "Wrigleyville." As Americans' habits changed and the Cubs grew more popular, the area did not grow more appreciably hospitable to the private car. That is why today those who insist on driving to the ballgame rather than taking the El train may be gouged $40 or even more for parking, or find themselves in the type of traffic jams only those fleeing war-torn Third World countries face.

The plush greenery of Wrigley's walls and seats and field are familiar characteristics, but part of its uniqueness is owed to the annual planting and growth of ivy on the outfield walls. During the late 1920s and early 1930s, William Wrigley's right-hand man was William Veeck Sr. Bill Veeck Jr., regarded as the most creative owner-entrepreneur during his subsequent half-century front-office career in St. Louis and with the White Sox, began working for the club as a very young man.

When William Wrigley died in 1932, his son Philip, or P.K., took over. He kept Bill Jr. on. In 1937 Veeck responded well when P.K. said he wanted a more woodsy "park" appearance. Veeck called more upon knowledge of outfield decorations elsewhere than his own green thumb to make the choice. Fenway Park, built in 1912, may be older and have the left-field Green Monster, but it does not have vegetation growing on the walls.

Players, too, gradually adopted the fans' view that Wrigley was a special place for baseball. Hall of Fame shortstop and first baseman Ernie Banks, the team's most popular player of all time for his achievements during his 1953 to 1971 career, never met a ballgame he didn't like, and is effusive about Wrigley.

"Most players will tell you that they would have given anything to play at Wrigley Field during the time I did," Banks said. "It's simply beautiful. The fans there and the ivy on the wall. I think people should take their shoes off when they go there."

Andre Dawson, who won the 1987 Most Valuable Player award while playing right field for the last-place Cubs that season, admires Wrigley just as much.

"I think there are a few special ballparks," said Dawson, who is now a special assistant to the president of the Florida Marlins. "They're numbered. There are only a few left. The fans are right on top of you. They're very involved."

When Dawson joined the Cubs in 1987, Wrigley was foremost in his mind. He knew the Cubs played no night games and he appreciated that the park had natural grass, not artificial turf—important because his knees were fragile. One by one, baseball has discarded the artificial turf surfaces it embraced so enthusiastically and returned fields from concrete hard to real-grass soft.

Not only are the fans on top of the action inside the park, Wrigley is the rare ballpark that offers first-rate views of the game from outside the park. Because the big-city neighborhood surrounds Wrigley, apartment buildings loom over the outfield walls. Crafty landlords have taken advantage by building sophisticated metal bleachers on their roofs and charging admission.

For a park praised as the epitome of major league baseball class—with banners of retired stars waving in the ground-level concourse and flags representing significant retired figures in franchise history waving outside—it is curious and somewhat tacky to gaze out from behind home plate toward left field. The viewer is confronted by a building's red roof transformed into a Budweiser beer ad. Nothing is sacred and there is no respite from hype in the modern age, but it does nothing for the Wrigley ambience.

Although the outside viewing tradition goes back decades, understandably, Cubs officials and club owner, the Tribune Company, which owns the *Chicago Tribune*, are peeved. They see the situation a little bit like the auto owner who fills his gas tank and then sees the product siphoned off. While the Cubs would like nothing better than to build gigantic walls that would obstruct the sight lines, the mayor and city council would never approve. There have been numerous battles over the rights to the view.

Remarkably, such contention even predates the existence of Wrigley Field. In 1899 a make-a-buck–inclined fellow named Andrew Brennan

TOP TEN

Cubs Single-Season Batting Averages (since 1900)

	Name	Year	Batting Average
1.	Rogers Hornsby	1929	.380
2.	Heinie Zimmerman	1912	.372
3.	Riggs Stephenson	1929	.362
4.	Kiki Cuyler	1929	.360
5.	Hack Wilson	1930	.356
6.	Kiki Cuyler	1930	.355
7.	Phil Cavarretta	1945	.355
8.	Ray Grimes	1922	.354
9.	Bill Madlock	1975	.354
10.	Hack Miller	1922	.352

DID YOU KNOW . . . That any player who hit home runs in double figures in a season before 1920 was considered a slugger? Frank Schulte's 21 in 1911 was the all-time team best until Gabby Hartnett hit 24 in 1925.

lived in a home across the street from the West Side Grounds. He built seats on the roof and began selling them. The appalled Cubs went to court, but a judge ruled in favor of Brennan's right to sell the seats. Other building owners followed his lead, but in 1908 a spectator died after falling off a roof and the city condemned many of the buildings.

However, the practice resumed later and by the early 2000s the Cubs were in court once again, essentially claiming that the landlords were stealing their product. It is difficult to argue that the rooftop seats are actually better than those in the park, but with the Cubs' high rate of sell-outs, their availability does expand the viewing audience.

Tickets at about a dozen buildings on Sheffield and Waveland Avenues facing the field go for $100 to $150 each, far more than most regularly priced tickets, but do include unlimited supplies of beer, brats, and hot dogs. Some applaud the free enterprise nature of the owners, who are often regarded as the little guy fighting the big corporation, albeit with city hall on their side. Others flatly consider the landlords thieves, stealing from another's business.

Ultimately, the Cubs and the landlords cut a deal, ending the most recent court case with an agreement in 2005 that the apartment owners will fork over 17 percent of their revenue to the team. Truce declared.

The Cubs are a Chicago civic institution. To some extent, so is the *Chicago Tribune*, which was founded in 1847. And one might say that is also true of the Daley family. Mayor Richard J. Daley was a renowned figure in the city's history. Current mayor Richard M. Daley, his son, is credited with beautifying and upgrading the community. However, quite frequently political controversies put the mayor and the newspaper at loggerheads.

So in the summer of 2004 when chunks of concrete began falling from the overhang into seats at Wrigley Field, the present Mayor Daley seemed almost gleeful about going to battle with the Tribune over the issues of building inspection and repairs.

By the NUMBERS .339—Adrian "Cap" Anson, who retired in 1897, still owns the all-time Cubs career batting average of .339. As a Cub, Anson is second in games played with 2,533, second in at-bats with 9,084, first in runs scored with 1,711, first in hits with 3,081, first in singles with 2,330, first in doubles with 530, and first in RBIs with 1,879.

It is no exaggeration to say that in late August of that year Chicken Little was right. The sky was falling. A brick-sized piece of concrete plummeted to the seats, just missing a fan. Then additional, larger pieces tore loose. Daley blustered about unsafe conditions, and the prospect was raised that 90-year-old Wrigley might be shut down temporarily. There was talk of moving remaining Cubs games to Milwaukee's Miller Park or to the White Sox' U.S. Cellular Field, alias Comiskey Park.

Painted in white across the top of the visitors' dugout on the third-base side are the words, "Welcome to the Friendly Confines of Wrigley Field." Just as the sarcastic have noted during dismal Cubs' seasons over the years that the park was not being too friendly, there was a brief period when spectators feared being crunched by falling hunks of the ballpark.

Once again peace eventually broke out when netting was placed under the overhangs to protect against falling objects and more significant repairs were undertaken and sanctioned in the off-season. Wrigley Field was patched and presumably regained its image as immortal.

Chicago is known as the Windy City, not as most people assume because of its strident breezes blowing ashore off Lake Michigan. The city's nickname was bestowed more than a hundred years ago in honor of its windy politicians. However, it is quite accurate to say that the wind blows in bizarre fashion at Wrigley. When teams come to the grounds, they often check to see if the wind is blowing in (favoring pitchers) or out (favoring hitters).

Sometimes, when the wind is blowing out at gale force, hitters feast and stuff happens. On August. 25, 1922, the Cubs bested the Philadelphia Phillies, 26–23 at Wrigley in the highest-scoring game ever. The box score included 51 hits, 21 walks, and 10 errors, so the strange doings cannot all be blamed on the meteorological conditions.

On April 17, 1976, the Phillies trailed by 11 runs before beating the Cubs 18–16 in ten innings at Wrigley. A few weeks later, on May 5, the Los

Angeles Dodgers slugged seven homers and topped the Cubs 14–12. The wind was blowing out 31 mph that day. In the press box, at the beginning of each game at Wrigley, the public address announcer is sure to inform the media of that day's wind velocity.

Amusingly, the Cubs' 2005 media guide included a small chart keeping track of the wind and the team's performance in various conditions. The previous season the Cubs went 16–19 with the wind blowing in and 26–13 with the wind blowing out. The team was 3–5 with a crosswind. It is not

A packed Wrigley Field for the 1947 All-Star Game. Built in 1914, Wrigley remains a distinguished, popular monument to the game.

immediately clear how that input helps General Manager Jim Hendry build a team, but maybe the club will employ someone to stand on the pitcher's mound, lick an index finger, and hold it up in the air. The fans, of course, would simply feel that the Cubs are proclaiming themselves number one.

From its inception until 1988, Wrigley Field also never witnessed anything but day baseball. The Cubs and the field were the last in the majors to adopt night games. Over the years many analysts suggested that the players failed to win pennants because the heat of the summer wore them out.

Yet for all its vagaries and challenges, Wrigley leaves some ballplayers misty-eyed. Ron Santo, the Cubs' star third-baseman from 1960 to 1973 and every bit as popular as Banks now that he is a long-time broadcaster, grew up in Seattle.

Once a week he was able to watch a National League game of the week on television. Even from a distance of 2,000 miles and through a filtering medium, Santo became enamored of Wrigley Field.

"Right there and then," Santo said, "there was something special. I don't know why, but there was just something I loved about that ballpark."

That love-at-first-sight impression was important. Santo was pursued by several big-league teams and he chose the Cubs even though they did not make the best offer. The image of Wrigley was lodged in his head. Then, when he made the big club, the first visit to Santo's new workplace was like a dream.

"I stepped on the grass at Wrigley Field, and even with nobody in the stands, I swear to God, I felt like I was walking on air," Santo said. "There was just something there. You know, I had seen it on TV, but this was nothing like that. I knew I was exactly in the right place."

More Good Old Days

After their early National League dominance ended with a loss to the Philadelphia Athletics in the 1910 World Series, the Cubs regrouped and returned to the Series in 1918.

Just as 1908 is a magic year in Cubs history, 1918 was a magic year in Boston Red Sox history. For 86 years it was referred to as the last time the Red Sox won the World Series. Who did they beat that season? The Cubs. The Red Sox ended their drought in 2004, but the Cubs are still hoping for a little rain.

Although generations of Cubs were raised believing their team was always a second-division club, that is due primarily to a failure to consult baseball encyclopedias. The Cubs had several other pre–World War II World Series opportunities. Not everyone, however, demonstrated Frank Chance's peerless leadership in the dugout, and management made some boneheaded decisions.

Rabbit Maranville was a colorful player and a shortstop of sufficient talent to be chosen for the Hall of Fame, but his 1925, two-month tenure as manager was worse than his 23–30 record implied. Whatever Maranville did provided wonderful fodder for surprised journalists, but little in the way of fatherly advice for younger players.

Maranville was a wild man who drank a little too much, partied a little too hard, and was less mature, on occasion, than a kindergartner. Once, Maranville darted through a train, splashing ice water on his players. Another time he sprayed train patrons with the contents of a spittoon. And good-natured Charlie Grimm was silly enough to join Maranville in a stunt taken too far.

The two agreed to pose for a picture. Grimm lay on his back with a golf tee in his mouth. Maranville stepped up to swing a club. He was supposed to pause just as the photograph was snapped. Well, the picture was taken, but Maranville followed through on his swing, teeing off Grimm's mouth. The shocked Grimm was as scared as he was angry. Soon enough, Maranville was canned.

Cubs shortstop Jimmy Cooney completed the rarest play in baseball, notching an unassisted triple play on May 30, 1927, in a 7–6 win over the Pirates in Pittsburgh. With runners on first and second, Cooney caught a line drive off the bat of future Hall of Famer Lloyd Waner, stepped on

Although he was a terrific ballplayer, Rabbit Maranville had a brief, checkered tenure as Cubs manager. He alienated players, was rowdy in public, and drove the team crazy.

second base catching Lloyd's brother Paul for the second out, and then tagged Clyde Barnhart as he ran toward him.

Eight days later, the Cubs traded Cooney to the Phillies. Cynical fans in later years would say, "That's so Cubs." The phrase was commonly uttered when the team's actions baffled fans.

The Cubs were taken over by the anti-Maranville, the fabulous second baseman Rogers Hornsby, who was more sour than businesslike, more dour than frivolous. Hornsby's personality wore thin, and by 1929 Joe McCarthy was in charge, coaxing a great season out of the club, even if the Cubs lost to Philadelphia four games to one in the Series.

The team set a Major League attendance record of 1,485,166 fans, a mark that stood until 1946 and a team record that lasted for 40 years. Hornsby batted .380 that year; Riggs Stephenson, .362; and Kiki Cuyler, .360. The dead-ball era was a distant memory.

The World Series was a bitter one. Two great backstops, Mickey Cochrane of the A's and Charles Leo "Gabby" Hartnett, indeed were gabby. Hartnett insulted Cochrane from the get-go, calling him a "county fair catcher."

When Hartnett took a called strike early in a game, Cochrane waved the ball in his face and said, "See that? That's the thing you're supposed to hit!"

On strike two, he taunted Hartnett with, "You supposed to be a hitter?"

On strike three, he added, "Back to the bushes, you county fair catcher."

Such enmity was unusual for Hartnett, but he missed most of the year with an arm injury and was possibly in a season-long funk.

Some of the all-time best Cubs were on the roster in 1929, and center fielder Hack Wilson prefaced his astonishing 1930 season by smacking 39 home runs, driving in 159 and hitting .345. Wilson was a chunky, 5'6" power hitter who a year later clubbed 56 homers. That remained the National League record until 1998, when Mark McGwire and Sammy Sosa eclipsed Roger Maris' major league mark. Wilson's 191 RBIs that season has never been topped and is hardly ever approached.

For nearly 70 years, Wilson's RBI record was recognized at 190. However, a 1999 evaluation of box scores by official baseball historian Jerome Holtzman, the former Chicago baseball writer, credited Wilson

TOP TEN

Cubs Career Wins for Pitchers

	Name	Wins
1.	Charlie Root	201
2.	Mordecai "Three Finger" Brown	188
3.	Bill Hutchison	180
4.	Larry Corcoran	175
5.	Ferguson Jenkins	167
6.	Guy Bush	152
7.	Clark Griffith	152
8.	Hippo Vaughn	151
9.	Bill Lee	139
10.	John Clarkson	137

with an overlooked RBI. Commissioner Bud Selig approved the change.

Wilson is one of the greatest of Cubs, but his is among the most tragic of stories. He lapped up the adulation from his phenomenal season, began drinking heavily, gained 20 pounds, and never came close to matching his 1930 success.

Grimm, who as a player, coach, manager, and broadcaster had a half-century association with the Cubs and was known as "Jolly Cholly" for his pleasant disposition, left-handed banjo playing, and crooning, said that Wilson may have been a drinker but it never interfered with his play.

"I never saw Wilson unfit to play," Grimm said. "Hungover, yes, but never not ready to hit. Gad, that little man would murder that ball to right-center."

Before Wilson died in 1948, he appeared on a TV program in which he poignantly admitted that more than talent is necessary to succeed in baseball.

"Things like good advice and common sense," Wilson said.

Remembering arguments with managers and other teammates, he subsequently conceded that as a player he had not lived up to that standard.

"I was quite a guy back in those days," Wilson said. "I had a lot of natural talent. I sure lacked a lot of other things, like humility and

Slugging Hack Wilson had an astonishingly productive 1930 season, with 56 home runs and a still-standing major league record of 191 RBIs. Sadly, Wilson's career quickly came to an end because of his drinking and partying.

IF ONLY . . . Lewis Robert "Hack" Wilson had been a teetotaler. He only played 12 years in the majors, including three seasons in which he played less than half his team's games. Although he was elected to the Hall of Fame in 1979 with a lifetime .307 average and 244 home runs, imagine what his statistics—and his life—would have been like had he not succumbed to heavy drinking.

common sense. Baseball came so easy to me that I thought the whole world was my oyster. Hack Wilson knew everything. It didn't catch up to me for a while."

In 1939 Wilson, who made a top salary of $40,000, admitted being "flat broke." When he showed up in bars, some insulted him, calling him a bum. He bristled at that.

"I'm no bum," Wilson said. "Yeah, I made a lot of mistakes when I was in the chips. But I don't regret a one of them. They were expensive mistakes, but I had a lot of laughs."

The great slugger Hack Wilson was only 48 when he died.

The Roaring '30s

It was one of the most famous plays in baseball history—and no one knows for sure what happened.

The old mythmaker himself, Babe Ruth, was at the root of the story, and a man named Root was a key protagonist. The matter, of course, revolves around the home run the Sultan of Swat hit during the fifth inning of the third game of the 1932 World Series.

The Cubs returned to the classic amidst a backdrop of bad feeling between Yankees manager Joe McCarthy and Chicago owner William Wrigley. McCarthy was the skipper of the Cubs in 1929 when they last visited the World Series, but was fired anyway. In a singular misjudgment in his dismissal of one of the game's greatest field leaders, Wrigley explained that McCarthy would never lead his Cubs to a world championship. Now there was McCarthy in the other dugout.

McCarthy looked quite competent at the helm, leading the Yankees to 107 victories, watching hitters such as Lou Gehrig, Earle Combs, Tony Lazzeri, Bill Dickey, and Ruth light it up, and pitchers such as Lefty Gomez, Herb Pennock, and Red Ruffing pile up the wins. It was too late for a Wrigley do-over.

The Yankees took the first two games of the Series. At their hotel in Chicago, the team was subjected to considerable unruly, classless fan abuse. Ruth and his wife had a bag of water thrown at them. Like any great champion, it was never wise to irritate Ruth. He clubbed a three-run homer in the first inning.

When he came to bat in the fifth, there was one out. The Wrigley fans, likely incited by the earlier homer, became even more vociferous than usual, booing Ruth with vigor. It is here, despite more than 30,000 eyewitnesses, that stories diverge. Some say Ruth took a fastball for a

Outfielder Kiki Cuyler wielded a potent bat for the Cubs between 1928 and 1935, contributing at a time when the club made regular appearances in the World Series. Photo courtesy of National Baseball Hall of Fame Library, Cooperstown, New York.

strike from Charlie Root and then pointed to the center-field bleachers. Then he took a second strike, motioning with his fingers, "That's two." On the next pitch, a Root fastball, Ruth swung and powdered the ball for another homer, putting it almost precisely where he had pointed in center field.

That's one side of it. Root always contended that if Ruth showboated like that he would have stuck a pitch in his ear. Many newspaper accounts of the game made no report of any so-called "called shot," as the play entered the lexicon. Ruth was cagey at first when asked if he had called the homer, but as time passed, the Bambino, never shy in the spotlight, let on that indeed he had.

There are photographs with Ruth seemingly pointing to something. Some say the gesture indicates that, yes, he had called the big hit. Others say

TRIVIA

Have any members of the Cubs who participated in at least 100 games in a season ever fielded 1.000?

Answers to the trivia questions are on pages 158–159.

he was pointing at something else. There was no television coverage with instant replay in 1932. However, 67 years later, a spectator named Harold Warp surfaced and claimed that the only baseball game he attended in his life was the third game of the 1932 World Series, and, oh by the way, he shot 16mm film of the event on that October 1.

The film showed Ruth doing something with his hand that could be interpreted as pointing, hitting a home run, and then raucously circling the bases making fun of Root, the Cubs, and the fans. Not being much of a baseball fan but more of a chronicler of family events, Warp let the film sit around unexamined for more than 60 years. After he died in 1994, family members realized that it was possibly an important piece of film and baseball history, and it was shown on ESPN.

Did Ruth truly call his shot, announcing to the world that he was going to slug a home run? The bravado it took to do such a thing matched his personality and likely his mood of the moment. Can it be stated unequivocally that he did? No. But it is possible, and it is a wonderful baseball yarn that all but Cubs players and fans would prefer to believe.

Oh, yes, the Yankees did sweep the Cubs that October, four games to zip.

Ruth's home run and the hoopla surrounding it is one of baseball's memorable plays, but it was not the wackiest story featuring the Cubs that season. Under the heading of "What We Do for Love," on July 6 of that summer, shortstop Billy Jurges was shot with a .25 caliber pistol by a former actress girlfriend. He was hit in the ribs, shoulder, and left hand, but only missed 17 days of playing time. Jurges chose not to press charges because he thought she didn't really mean to shoot him. Now that's a fellow who is an optimist. The woman incorporated the incident into her act, and the story loosely parallels what befalls the character of Roy Hobbs in Bernard Malamud's novel *The Natural* (later a movie starring Robert Redford). However, it is said that the real-life circumstance that Malamud took the situation from in his book was the shooting of player Eddie Waitkus by another woman some two decades later.

Jurges, who later in life managed the Boston Red Sox, seemingly engaged in more fistfights than Muhammad Ali. Alas, Jurges' were unsanctioned, and often over trifling matters. The man had a temper. In July of the 1935 season, Jurges refought the Civil War. A northerner from Brooklyn, Jurges and teammate Walter Stephenson, who was from North Carolina, duked it out in the dugout following Jurges' disparagement of the Confederacy.

Another time the persistent Jurges kicked dirt on home plate five times after being tossed from a game.

In general the 1930s were fairly good to the Cubs. They could count on winning the pennant every few years—1932, 1935, and 1938—and then losing the World Series.

One of the decade's greats was center fielder Kiki Cuyler. Cuyler, however, missed the first two weeks of the 1934 season from an infected hangnail caused by his own clubhouse manicure. This would indicate there is nothing really new in the game, as more than 60 years later, Sammy Sosa would suffer a similar nail indignity and also was sidelined with a back injury when he sneezed too hard.

In the early 1930s, new owner P. K. Wrigley could not be persuaded to sign Joe DiMaggio. He worried about a DiMaggio knee injury and even refused

TRIVIA

Who was the first Cubs player to win the Most Valuable Player award, and what was the award called at the time?

Answers to the trivia questions are on pages 158–159.

That in 1930, the year of the hitter, the Cubs' staff earned-run average was a horrid 4.80? However, it was not the worst in team history. In 1894 the pitchers' ERA was 5.63. And in 1999 (5.27) and 2000 (5.25), it was also astonishingly high.

a money-back guarantee. That is possibly the worst personnel decision in franchise history.

The Cubs of the 1930s featured Stan Hack at third base, Cuyler, Hartnett, and Billy Herman. Jerome Holtzman, a 10-year-old during the time period, made his first acquaintanceship with the Cubs before beginning his Hall of Fame sportswriting career in the 1940s. Holtzman got to know Grimm, who kept popping back into the Cubs picture in one capacity or another, a little bit better in later years.

"He had a beer garden baritone," said Holtzman, who wrote sports for the *Chicago Sun-Times* and *Chicago Tribune* from the 1940s through the 1990s and said he wished he had worked one day in the 2000s. Holtzman's final 40-plus years in the business emphasized baseball coverage. "He [Grimm] played 'Lazy River,' 'Peg of my Heart,' and 'Oh, Susanna.'"

It is no mystery to Holtzman why the top-notch Cubs teams of the 1930s are not better remembered.

"There aren't too many people alive from the 1930s," he said.

The Cubs of 1935 reached still another World Series that ended in frustration, losing four games to two to the Detroit Tigers. They were on fire down the stretch, winning 21 straight games, the second longest winning streak in major league history. The Cubs conquered September but once again could not triumph in October.

Easygoing manager Charlie Grimm went ballistic in that series. Grimm was heaved from the pivotal third game. The Series was tied 1–1, with the game knotted at 3–3, and then 5–5. The Cubs lost 6–5 in the eleventh inning, on a single, an error, and a single. Close calls vexed Grimm, and when the Cubs went down in the Series, he blamed umpire George Moriarty.

"Moriarty cost us the Series," Grimm said. "I don't question his honesty. I say he is prejudiced, which is worse. A crooked umpire will try to even things up and cover his crookedness, but Moriarty had what we call a 'redneck' all through. He was an angered madman, foaming and cursing us constantly.

"Say, with $300,000 at stake, a manager has the right to protest a decision, hasn't he? When did you last hear of a manager getting heaved out of a World Series?"

These days Grimm might have been fined $300,000 by the commissioner for shooting off his mouth like that. It was an ungracious display by a normally gracious man.

From Merkle's Boner to Ruth's called shot, the Cubs always seemed to find themselves on the highlight tape of baseball's most controversial plays. So it should be no surprise that the so-called "Homer in the Gloamin'" involved the Cubs at the end of the 1938 season.

The Cubs were mixing it up with the Pittsburgh Pirates on September 28. It was 5–5 in the bottom of the ninth inning when Gabby Hartnett came to the plate. Darkness was settling fast on the park with

A Cubs "murderers' row" of sorts. From left to right, Billy Herman, Billy Jurges, Frank DeMaree, and catcher Gabby Hartnett, who also managed the team after his playing days were over.

IF ONLY . . . Plate umpire Bruce Froemming had called strike three. There were two outs in the ninth inning and Cubs right-hander Milt Pappas had not allowed a base runner versus the San Diego Padres on September 2, 1972. A 3–2 pitch to Larry Stahl—that many thought was over the plate—was called ball four and ruined a perfect game. Pappas completed the no-hitter.

no lights. The umpires had already decided the game would not go into extra innings. So if the Cubs, who had two outs, did not score, the game would end.

Hartnett, who by then was also manager, relieving Charlie Grimm, swung at an 0–2 pitch thrown by Mace Brown and smashed a barely visible home run. The ball landed in the left-field stands, though through the thickening gloom the spectators pretty much called the home run. Fans rushed the field, hugging the hitter, and Hartnett had to fight his way around the bases to touch home plate. The win pushed the Cubs one-half game ahead of the Pirates into first place. The remarkable blow propelled the Cubs into the World Series for the third time in the decade.

Not surprisingly, when reflecting on his career, Hartnett called the Homer in the Gloamin' his biggest thrill.

The Cubs met the Yankees in the Series. Chicago lost the opener at home, and when Dizzy Dean was chosen to start Game 2, he promised Hartnett, "I'll flatten 'em, Leo." Dean was a charter member of the St. Louis Cardinals' Gashouse Gang and figured to put up some of the greatest pitching numbers of all-time until he was injured in the All-Star Game. The Cubs picked him up, hoping he could regain his form. Dean, who as a broadcaster gained equal renown as in his playing days, was prone to say anything that came into his mind. Alas, he could not make good on the pledge, and the Yankees were victorious, on their way to a four-game sweep.

After the second loss, Hartnett said, "We still are looking for our first break."

Millions of Cubs fans have echoed the sentiment in the years since.

Amusingly, the Series was so popular that the *New York Daily News* had to plead with readers not to phone the office for mid-game updates. A small item in the October 7 paper demanded attention: "Please Don't Call," it read. "Please do not call The News for World Series scores as it overtaxes our switchboard and interferes with necessary business. Watch the Pink and later editions for first-hand results of the game."

A follow-up announcement a day later reading, "We told you not to call" could not be found. Possibly everyone went back to the Internet after the stern warning.

Grimm, who was born in 1898, was always affable and flexible. He played in the majors for 20 years and ended his career in 1939 with a lifetime .290 batting average. Subsequently, he managed the Cubs five different times over a 30-year period. He was known for his joke-telling, as well as singing German songs and playing his banjo. Grimm's mother played harmonica, his father played the fiddle, one brother played the mandolin, and another brother played guitar.

Later in life, Grimm was tapped to sell Quench gum by a friend, but he asked Wrigley, the chewing gum baron, for permission before taking the job. Wrigley was surprised, but said it was okay.

"Go ahead," Wrigley said. "You won't hurt me."

Wrigley knew what he was talking about when it came to the gum trade, and he was right on with that prognosis.

The Other Guys in Town

Cubs manager Dusty Baker did not pretend, did not utter the typical coach quote that "it's just another game." Nope. Sitting in the home dugout at Wrigley Field on a hot summer's evening a few days before the Cubs were scheduled to play the Chicago White Sox in their second three-game series of the 2005 season, he spoke the truth.

"You feel it's not just another game," Baker said. "It's a little more intense than that. You see how important it is to the town, to families and businesses."

In the early days of Major League Baseball, when leagues came and went, franchises were born and died, or later moved on, there were multiple teams in cities like New York, Boston, Philadelphia, and Chicago. But the century-long shakedown, population growth in different regions of the United States, and economic realities have left fans with really just two cities thriving with two teams. There are the Yankees and Mets in New York and the Cubs and White Sox in Chicago. There are also the Dodgers in Los Angeles and the Angels of Los Angeles/Anaheim/Disneyland, separated by something like 50 miles of might-as-well-be-impenetrable traffic. They sort of represent the same city.

The Cubs and White Sox, however, are into 105 years of soul separation. Those who grow up as baseball fans in other parts of the nation mostly think, "How cool. They have two teams. If I lived there I could go to both American League and National League games whenever I wanted to."

Logical, huh? Nah. Most people in Chicago do not think like that. Sometimes it is difficult to tell if White Sox fans are happier when their team wins or the Cubs lose. There is a great divide. Choices of who to support were bred into families generations ago. There is also a

TRIVIA

In which year did the Cubs first place numbers on the backs of their uniforms?

Answers to the trivia questions are on pages 158–159.

geographical divide. Those from the South Side are White Sox backers. Those from the North Side are Cubs backers. You might call the Loop the Mason-Dixon line separating baseball fans.

The joke goes that the only thing the Cubs and White Sox have in common is the Chicago Transit Authority's Red Line El train. The Red Line delivers fans to both parks. Go south to 35th Street/Sox Park for the White Sox and go north to Addison for Wrigley.

Certainly there are numerous fans who retain a sense of sanity, who will root, root, root for their team first and foremost but, as Chicagoans, be happy for the success of the other team as long as it does not come at the expense of their team.

Such squishy sentiments go down the drain, though, on the occasions when the Cubs and White Sox meet. And under one guise or another, they have played each other more often than most fans might think.

The most significant encounter, of course, was in the 1906 World Series, when the heavily favored, 116 game–winning Cubs lost to the White Sox. That is the only time the two Chicago teams have played in the postseason.

Yet in most years between 1903 and 1942, the clubs engaged in a postseason City Series. The games didn't count in the standings, but were taken very seriously. From the 1940s to the 1990s, the Cubs and White Sox contested exhibition games.

"It was just to satisfy the fans," said Cubs Hall of Fame outfielder Billy Williams, who played in his share. "You separate the fans when you play that game."

And then, in 1997, Major League Baseball introduced interleague play. Clearly, a regular Cubs–White Sox series had to be a staple of that type of schedule, and indeed planners have been quite conscious of shifting games back and forth between Wrigley Field and Comiskey Park/U.S. Cellular Field.

The first interleague meeting took place June 16, 1997, at Comiskey, and the Cubs won 8–3. That was the first of a three-game series in the American League team's park. In 1998 the teams played three games at

Wrigley. But starting in 1999 each club hosted a three-game series each season.

As long as the teams were going to play interleague games, it made sense to play an equal number at each team's park each year. The games quickly became highlights on the schedule and sold out every game. This equality of distribution is especially important for committed White Sox fans, who usually think their team is slighted in favor of the Cubs routinely by the media, the city, the baseball world, and upscale, trendy fans. The paranoia emerges regularly, but with equality of scheduling, there is no room for griping.

In the past, it was not uncommon for players to become rooted in the communities where they played as regular fixtures in the lineup. They became part of the culture of the team and the supporters. Players move around from team to team much more frequently now, but they do transfer allegiances as quickly as they change uniform jerseys. So if a player is wearing an outfit that reads "White Sox" and he has experienced any Cubs buzz, he understands the emotion attached to the matchups.

The 1906 Chicago Cubs team picture. That team won a record 116 games, equaled by the Seattle Mariners nearly a century later, but never topped. Yet the Cubs were upset by the Chicago White Sox in the World Series.

Cubs retired jersey numbers:

10—Ron Santo

14—Ernie Banks

23—Ryne Sandberg

26—Billy Williams

42—Retired by all major league teams to honor Jackie Robinson

"It's cool," said White Sox catcher A. J. Pierzynski in the summer of 2005. "It's definitely a fun series. It definitely gives you an extra kick."

Players enjoy competing in front of full houses, when the sound is magnified and every little move on the field stokes the crowd.

"You get into it," said White Sox outfielder Jermaine Dye. "It seems like a playoff atmosphere."

Whether they picked up the vibes in Little League, high school, or college, most players step into a local rivalry at some point in their athletic careers where almost instantly they can sense that "this one is different."

Former White Sox center fielder Aaron Rowand called the series "a crosstown rivalry. It's something we look forward to."

The results may not be as critical to the season's standings as an Auburn-Alabama college football game or a Bears-Packers National Football League game, but that bragging rights thing attaches itself to Cubs–White Sox in the same way.

"The fans elevate it," said outfielder Todd Hollandsworth, a Cub from 2004 to 2005. "They jump on it. They make you want to run with it. It's huge for the fans. For us, it's a game we've got to win."

As so often occurs in rivalry games, whether it be Michigan–Ohio State in football or Oklahoma–Oklahoma State in anything, how the teams were faring during the regular season meant nothing once the Cubs–White Sox series began.

Between 1997 and 2004, the Cubs went 20–22 against the White Sox. What happened in 2005 over six games, going back and forth on the Red Line? The teams split, 3–3, and the White Sox still lead the all-time series, now 25–23.

The Curse Makes It Worse

The Billy Goat Tavern is best known nationwide as the restaurant in *Saturday Night Live* skits where the workers chant, "Cheeseborger, cheeseborger, cheeseborger," and repeat, "No Coke, Pepsi."

The main branch is located in downtown Chicago, on Lower Michigan Avenue, just a few steps from where many newspaper scribes work. It has long been a favorite hangout for reporters. The late, great columnist Mike Royko was close to the owners, often dining on the premises.

By the time the 1945 World Series rolled around, the Cubs had been idle in October for seven years. Billy Goat owner Bill Sianis decided that his nanny goat Senovia should have the privilege of attending one of the games at Wrigley Field against the Tigers. He bought two tickets, but on game day Sianis was refused admission unless he left Senovia at home.

Asked why he couldn't bring the goat to the game, Sianis was told, "The goat smells."

Incensed, Sianis issued his famous curse. In retaliation for Senovia being barred, Sianis engaged in a type of voodoo. He proclaimed that in retaliation for their actions against him and his pet, the Cubs would never play in another World Series.

The Red Sox had the Curse of the Bambino. Although Babe Ruth did not suggest the Red Sox would never win another World Series after owner Harry Frazee sold him to the New York Yankees in 1920, the fortunes of the two teams diverged mightily from that moment. Ruth led the Yankees to championship after championship, and the team became the winningest in sports over the decades, perpetuating its dominance for more than 80 years.

First baseman Phil Cavarretta, who was still a teenager when he joined the Cubs, was the Most Valuable Player in the National League in 1945, the last time the Cubs reached the World Series. Photo courtesy of National Baseball Hall of Fame Library, Cooperstown, New York.

Supposedly, Frazee used the proceeds from the sale of Ruth to pay bills and finance the Broadway show *No, No, Nanette*. This galled Red Sox fans even more, especially as the long years dragged by without a World Series championship. Periodically, the Red Sox slipped through to the Series, carried it out to the seventh game, and broke hearts by losing in the end. Finally, in 2004, they ended 86 years of frustration by defeating the St. Louis Cardinals in the World Series.

TRIVIA

Which future western television star played briefly for the Cubs during the 1951 season?

Answers to the trivia questions are on pages 158–159.

Cubs' frustration was truly just starting in 1945. The team went 98–56 and took the National League flag before falling to the Tigers four games to three. The season's most inspiring play was recorded by first baseman Phil Cavarretta.

Cavarretta played with the Cubs between 1934, when he was 18, and 1953. In 1945 he batted .355 and won the Most Valuable Player award; he also batted .423 in the Series. Cavarretta grew up in Chicago, so it was a thrill to be signed by his hometown team. In high school, while attending Lane Tech, Cavarretta sneaked into Wrigley Field with friends to watch games by climbing the right-field fence. He even played for the Cubs' Peoria team in the minors.

"First game as a pro and he hit for the cycle," long-time Cubs broadcaster Jack Brickhouse said. "Single, double, triple, and home run. What a way to break in."

Cavarretta also hit a home run in his first Cubs game as a starting player. Reaching the majors at such a young age, Cavarretta said he relied heavily on the advice of veteran second baseman Billy Herman. Eventually, Cavarretta became player/manager from 1951 to 1953.

In 1945 one grandstand ticket for a World Series game at Wrigley Field cost $18.35. The high livers might splurge for the box seats at $21.95. A miscommunication about housing in Detroit found Cavarretta and his wife in a pinch. A shortage of rooms exiled the couple in favor of a drummer from Grand Rapids who was in for the Series festivities and had a reservation. The Cavarrettas were prepared to spend the night in the hotel's lobby lounge, but were rescued. A Cubs fan, who knew a

TOP TEN
Cubs Career Shutouts

	Name	Shutouts
1.	Mordecai "Three Finger" Brown	48
2.	Hippo Vaughn	35
3.	Ed Reulbach	31
4.	Ferguson Jenkins	29
5.	Orval Overall	28
6.	Bill Lee	25
7.	Grover Alexander	24
8.	Claude Passeau	22
9.	Larry French	21 t
	Charlie Root	21 t

friend of a bellboy's second cousin (or something like that), found the Cavarrettas a hotel room.

Living in the Atlanta area late in life, Cavarretta regularly watched the Cubs on cable TV. He expressed amazement at the capabilities of Randy Johnson, Greg Maddux, and Roger Clemens, once praising Clemens as a throwback-style pitcher who seemed as "mean as an alligator."

Cavarretta, who played 22 seasons in all, finishing up with the White Sox, said modern players are in better shape than the 1940s and 1950s guys were and have better equipment. He said it was hard to move across town, and as soon as he retired he went right back to cheering for the Cubs.

"I'm still a Cub," Cavarretta said when he was 77. "Always was, always will be."

He also joked that he would give it a try if the Cubs wanted him to take another swing in their behalf.

"I think I could still make contact," Cavarretta said, "as long as you didn't throw it faster than 22 miles per hour."

Cavarretta's best year was a good year for baseball. World War II was ending, players were being discharged from the service and returning to their old teams. Fans, so long distracted by the horrors of battles from Pearl Harbor to Japan to Europe, began focusing on their old town teams once more.

A young center fielder on that team, brought up in 1943, emerged as a key player. Andy Pafko, born Andrew Pruschka in Boyceville, Wisconsin, in 1921, batted .298 with 110 RBIs that season. When he was deposited at third base later, manager Charlie Grimm's trust in his fielding led to Pafko being labeled "Handy Andy."

Pafko, who lives in Mount Prospect, Illinois, a Chicago suburb, had a blast that season.

"We were battling the Cardinals, as usual, and then we clinched the pennant in Pittsburgh," Pafko said.

Given that the Cubs swept a record 20 doubleheaders that season, it was appropriate that the pennant win occurred during a doubleheader. It was the first game at Wrigley on September 29, and Pafko made the difference in the 4–3 win.

"I drove in the winning run with a fly ball to right field and that did it for us," he said. "That clinched the pennant and then, of course, that got us into the World Series. So we had a wonderful evening that night. We had a little party. Charlie Grimm bought some champagne. That's the first time I ever tasted champagne."

Pafko, whose career also took him to the World Series for Brooklyn and Milwaukee, said Grimm was his favorite manager.

"He was quite a guy," Pafko said. "I played for a lot of great managers. He played his banjo. We played old songs together. We had a lot of fun. If you were a winning team you got to be like a happy family and to pull for each other. We had a lot of harmony. We loved each other like family."

The Cubs had been absent from the World Series since 1938, so Pafko felt lucky to be in one as a Cub. When the Cubs lost Game 2 to Tigers hurler Virgil Trucks, one headline read, Run Over by a Trucks. In the third game, the Cubs Claude Passeau pitched a gem and Tigers infielder Eddie Mayo said his slider "broke like a hummingbird."

Owner P. K. Wrigley showed up for Game 6 at Wrigley without a ticket, and dedicated usher "One-Eyed" Connolly said he couldn't come in. Wrigley

TRIVIA

At the end of which decade did the Cubs record a combined losing record for the first time?

Answers to the trivia questions are on pages 158–159.

pulled rank and not only did he witness the game, Connolly was fired. P. K. Wrigley picked off a goat and an usher in the same series.

Chicago did lose it all to Detroit in the seventh game.

"I'll never forget that one," said Pafko, who was 84 at the time he spoke. "We lost in the last game. The bases were loaded and a guy by the name of Paul Richards, who was a catcher in those days, hit a double down the left-field line. It cleared the bases and we never came back. But that was my first World Series, so that's the one I'll never forget."

Manager Charlie Grimm wasn't happy about losing, but apparently he wasn't dangerously distraught, either.

"I'm not going to hang myself," he said afterward.

Pafko was traded to the Dodgers during the 1951 season and he was unhappy about that. The Dodgers were in Chicago, and Pafko was standing around the batting cage before the game when Brooklyn pitcher Don Newcombe saw him.

"Don Newcombe, the big pitcher, hollers out, 'Hey, Pafko, you're going to be a Dodger tomorrow!'" Pafko recalled. "I guess there were rumors around New York. My name was mentioned in trades in New York that I was not aware of. And sure enough, I got home after the game, and my wife made dinner, and the phone rang. It was the general manager, and he said, 'Andy, I'm sorry to inform you, but we made an eight-player trade today with the Dodgers and you're a Dodger tomorrow.'"

Pafko met his wife in Chicago and felt it was home. His wife started to cry when he told her they were moving at the end of the series.

"I go up to my dressing room, take all of my stuff out, walk across the diamond, and play against my teammates the very next day," Pafko said. "You don't mind being traded in the off-season when you have time to adjust, but think about it: here I am a Cub one day and tomorrow I'm a Dodger."

Pafko played on the 1952 Dodgers World Series team and then was traded to the Braves and appeared in two more World Series before retiring in 1959.

"I came home to my home state to finish my career," Pafko said. "So I've been very fortunate."

The genial Andy Pafko, a first-rate outfielder for the Cubs and a member of the 1945 World Series team, won World Series rings with other teams later, but still lives in the Chicago suburbs and prefers to wear his Cubs ring. Photo courtesy of National Baseball Hall of Fame Library, Cooperstown, New York.

Pafko is as much a Cub in the 2000s as he was in the 1940s. He makes appearances at the annual winter Cubs Convention, and when Ernie Banks teases him, Pafko jabs back by showing off a World Series ring.

"I go, 'Ernie, by the way, how many of these do you have?'" Pafko said.

Although the 1957 Braves were champs, Pafko wears his Cubs World Series ring.

"I've got World Series everythings, but I wear my Cubs ring because that was my first one and I'm attached to that one, and it's a beautiful ring," Pafko said. "That's my first one and that's my favorite."

Pafko follows the team closely and still attends a small number of Cubs games each season. Although he has a lifetime major league pass to games around the country, he said the Cubs do a nice job of taking care of him any time he calls for tickets.

"They've got a good young club and they've got some young pitchers, so hopefully in the future they'll come around," Pafko said.

As a member of the last Cubs team to reach the World Series more than 60 years ago, Pafko has given some thought to how the city would react if the Cubs' turn comes around again.

"Gosh, I think the town would go wild," he said. "I tell you, I never saw a town, if anybody deserves a pennant, it's these wonderful fans. Win, lose, or draw they come out there in droves. A sellout every day. They really deserve a pennant with fans like that. I hope it's this year. If not, maybe next year. I hope it's in my lifetime."

A Cubs team in the World Series? That means beating the curse. Dusty Baker, who became manager in 2003, groans every time he hears the words "Billy Goat curse." He doesn't believe in it, doesn't want his players thinking about it, and if he had the power, he would probably take the last two goats on earth and ship them out on an ark with Noah. At the January 2004 Cubs Convention Baker was asked what his biggest surprise had been in Chicago after two seasons.

"The strength and magnitude of the goat," he said. "I've never seen an animal get this kind of recognition and power."

Didn't he ever hear of Lassie?

"We'd like to get rid of that goat," Baker said.

The Sianis family has tried to rectify the damage done by Bill Sianis. Sam Sianis, Bill Sianis' nephew, walked a goat through the turnstiles into Wrigley in 1984, 1989, 1993, 1998, and 2003 with no tangible results. If that's not curse-buster behavior, what is? There have been close calls, but no World Series. Maybe the goat needs a box seat and all the hot dogs and popcorn it can eat before the curse can be eradicated.

Tom Sianis, Bill Sianis' grand-nephew, said the clan has done its part to make up for the past.

"The Chicago Cubs," he said, "now it's their job."

Mr. Cub

If the phone rings and Ernie Banks is unable to pick up, the caller is greeted by this message: "Ernie Banks here. And how are you feeling?"

The sentiment is typical of the man who, during his 1953–1971 career as a shortstop and first baseman, came to be known as "Mr. Cub." The nickname was applied not only because of Banks' Hall of Fame credentials, but because of his ever-sunny, ever-cooperative attitude. Banks' signature phrase was, "Let's play two!"—meaning going out on the field for a doubleheader every day was fine with him.

Banks' legacy goes beyond his 512 home runs. He is described as "Nice Guy Ernie Banks" so frequently it is almost as if those words were etched on his birth certificate on January 31, 1931, in Dallas, Texas.

After Banks retired, Cubs owner P. K. Wrigley was asked if Banks might be considered as a future manager for the club.

"Why would Ernie want to be a manager?" Wrigley said. "It's the next thing to being a kamikaze pilot. He's too nice a guy."

Banks said Wrigley told that to him directly.

"I asked about managing," Banks said, "and he said managing is a tough business. I asked him, 'What process do you use to pick a manager?' He said, 'I don't know. I'll let you know.' He never did."

Did Banks ever really want to manage?

"No, sir," he said.

At various times, Banks said he did not have the temperament to be a manager. But his lack of interest in managing was not because he was tired of the game after he retired.

"You never get enough baseball," Banks said.

Banks was the stalwart slugger, the everyday leader on the field, the Cubs' best player, and the fans loved him for it. He never complained

"Mr. Cub" Ernie Banks, star at shortstop and first base for the Cubs in the 1950s and 1960s, holding the bat he used to swat his fifth grand slam of the 1955 season, against the St. Louis Cardinals. The Hall of Famer specialized in hitting four-baggers, with 512 for his career.

10,000—The Cubs, founded in 1876, became the first major league team to play 10,000 games in 1995, and won more than 50 percent of them, no doubt surprising to many.

when the team lost and sunk into last place. He always thought better times were coming. He always indicated he thought the next game, the next month, the next season, things would get better for the Cubs and their supporters. The attitude was ingrained in him, and it was really the same attitude the fans had. Neither the player nor the fan would give up. Someday, they knew, the Cubs would do it, would go all the way. And if they didn't do it right then, then the next time. It was no wonder that Banks was Mr. Cub. He represented all of the best in the franchise.

Banks predicted a pennant every season.

"I always believe," he said. "Some people think I don't. Some people think I should be in a lunatic asylum. But I say it every year and I believe it every year."

There were actually rumors in 1966 of a Banks trade, but P. K. Wrigley scotched them.

"Ernie started as a Cub, and that's what he'll always be," Wrigley said. "Today, tomorrow, next week, next year, and all of the years after that."

It's still true today.

Banks, whose "Let's play two" statement is worthy of *Bartlett's Familiar Quotations*, joked on a hazy, overcast night in Pittsburgh in 1967, "Lovely night to play three."

It was Jim Enright, a writer for the defunct *Chicago American*, who began calling Banks "Mr. Cub." Later, he wrote a book of the same name with Banks. Although no one else has ever doubted it, Banks wasn't sure the appendage fit.

"I told him, 'Jimmy, that's very nice of you, but I think we should kind of pass it on to other players and different players that join the Cubs,'" Banks said. "And he said, 'No, you're Mr. Cub.' And it stuck. It's a great thing and a lot of places I go people refer to me as 'Mr. Cub.' I see a lot of my contemporaries, Stan Musial, Al Kaline, Brooks Robinson, a lot of the guys from the Hall of Fame. There are a lot of nicknames—like Reggie Jackson is 'Mr. October.' They got 'Stan the Man' and all that. It's really nice to be called Mr. Cub. It's a pretty nice thing [to be] named after the team."

Banks was the first black player to break into the Cubs lineup. He had experience playing with the Kansas City Monarchs of the Negro National League and Buck O'Neil, the famed player and manager, steered him to Chicago. O'Neil, who became the first black major league coach with the Cubs, was often asked if he felt badly because he was too old to sign with the majors when the color barrier was broken. He usually said, "I was right on time," and later wrote a book with that title.

Sometimes, Banks says the same thing.

"My baseball life started at the right time," Banks said. "I was right on time. Kansas City Monarchs to Cubs."

The slow-to-embrace-change baseball owners permitted black players on major league teams for the first time in 1947. Jackie Robinson, under the guidance of Dodgers general manager Branch Rickey, took the heat for future generations. After a war against oppression, with black soldiers giving their lives in Europe and Japan during World War II, there was never a more advantageous time for Rickey's bold stroke. But if the Dodgers led the way, it was many years before all teams signed their first black player. The Boston Red Sox did not bring up Pumpsie Green until 1959.

The Cubs were neither pioneers nor slowpokes when they signed shortstop Gene Baker as their first black player. Banks, second to ink a contract, was the first to play in the majors when he made his debut on September 17, 1953. Banks went 0-for-3 in a loss to the Phillies at Wrigley Field. When Banks and Baker, stationed at second base, played together, they became the first black double-play combination in major league history.

Banks was the rare slugger at shortstop in the 1950s, a time when most shortstops were expected to field flawlessly, but were not counted on to do much more than hit their weight. In 19 seasons, Banks batted .274 with the 512 home runs and 1,636 RBIs. Playing on weak Cubs teams, Banks still won two Most Valuable Player awards in 1958 and 1959. Banks always carried a big stick, once hitting five grand-slam homers in a season.

The lanky Banks still has the National League record for home runs by a shortstop with 47 and held the Cubs record for most home runs by a first baseman with 37, until the 2005 season when Derrek Lee broke it. Lee said it was pretty special to find his name in the same sentence with Banks'.

"It's cool to be mentioned with Ernie, you know," Lee said. "I've gotten to know him. He's a great person. He doesn't really give me any advice about playing first base. It's more, 'Hi, how you doin'? What's going on?' That type of thing.

"He's definitely a fan. He loves the Cubs. He's a diehard. It's awesome."

Anyone who encounters Banks these days who never knew him would take away particular impressions. Has he always been this nice a person? And did he always talk so much? The answers are yes and yes.

In a 1969 interview, Banks said, "Am I ever grouchy? Well, I'm not going to say I jump out of bed every morning and start putting on my Cubs uniform while humming a tune. Sometimes I give myself a pep talk as I look into the mirror in the bathroom and tell myself I'm the luckiest guy alive."

In a cynical society, there might be suspicious minds who consider Banks' perpetually upbeat demeanor to be fraudulent or calculated. But those who knew him when he was playing say the Banks we see is the Banks they got. He always was genuine, optimistic, friendly, and gracious.

"That was always real," said Billy Williams, the Hall of Fame outfielder whose career with Banks on the Cubs overlapped for years. "A lot of people ask and say, 'Was he like this all the time?' And I don't hesitate to say he was because we roomed together for, like, a week-and-a-half at a time.

TRIVIA

Which Cubs manager has won the most games with the franchise?

Answers to the trivia questions are on pages 158–159.

"We got together after the game and did things before the game. We'd always sit and talk and I learned a lot about Ernie and the Negro League. I never did play in it, but he gave me a history of all the players who played in it and what they did as ballplayers."

Sportswriter Jerome Holtzman watched from the other side of the lines, but covered a large percentage of Banks' career with the Cubs.

"It was true that he never said a bad word about anybody," Holtzman said. "Not even Leo Durocher."

Durocher, the famous "Leo the Lip," known for his sarcasm and candid delivery, managed Banks near the end of his playing career, and the two did not get along.

IF ONLY ... Ken Hubbs hadn't been killed in February 1964 while piloting a small plane in a snowstorm in Utah. Hubbs burst onto the Chicago scene at second base as a 20-year-old in 1962 and won the National League Rookie of the Year award. At the end of the season, Hubbs initiated a triple play after catching a pop fly. A famous fielder, Hubbs looked like an infield fixture for years before his life was cut tragically short.

"Durocher was jealous of Banks," Holtzman said. "To him it was 'Mr. Cub, my ass.' Durocher used to criticize Banks. As an older player, Banks did not take a big lead off first. Durocher said he would buy him a suit of clothes if he just got picked off."

The manager, said Holtzman, would not say one good thing about the player most popular with the fans.

"One day in Philadelphia, in Connie Mack Stadium for a double-header, Banks had a great day," Holtzman said. "He hit three home runs, two home runs in the first game. The writers went down to the clubhouse between games and Durocher was asked, 'He had a hell of a game, didn't he?'

"And Durocher said, '[Glenn] Beckert had a hell of a game.'"

These days Banks will discourse on golf, a conversationalist's love life, the Nobel Peace Prize, hunting, fishing, just about anything. Fans did truly understand what a chatterbox Banks was on and off the field, during games and leading up to games.

"The first few years, you know, when we all come to the big leagues, we don't say that much," said Williams. "But once he started, man, you couldn't shut him up."

Banks' infield partner Glenn Beckert, who held down second base, said no one would believe how much Banks talked.

"He was just a remarkable fellow," said Beckert, who now lives in Florida. "Ernie, he could talk your legs off. I tell you, he comes up with more BS than I've ever heard. But a wonderful guy."

Once, not so long ago at one of the Cubs' winter conventions when old players come back to visit and greet fans, Beckert and Banks were both early arrivals.

"They have a cocktail reception on Friday and Ernie's sitting there in a corner, his knees were bothering him," Beckert said. "He said, 'Beck, I

By the
NUMBERS

12—The Cubs have had 12 players whose last names begin with Z. George Zabel, 1913–1915, Geoff Zahn, 1975–1976, Carlos Zambrano, 2001–present, Eduardo Zambrano, 1993–1994, Oscar Zamora, 1974–1976, Rollie Zeider, 1916–1918, Todd Zeile, 1995, Robert Zick, 1954, Don Zimmer, 1960–1961, Heinie Zimmerman, 1907–1916, Julio Zuleta, 2000–2001, Edward Zwilling, 1916.

want to talk to you. I want to tell you this. Glenn, learn to speak Japanese.' I said, 'What?' He said, 'Learn to speak Japanese. They're going to take over the world.' That was it."

The tidbit of advice came out of nowhere and left Beckert, who had no desire to enroll in Berlitz classes, befuddled. A couple of years later at a similar rendezvous Banks said, "Beck, I want to talk to you."

" 'What do you have this time, Ernie?' I ask. 'I'm going to have a baby.' I said, 'That's remarkable. You're 73 years old. I'd like to congratulate your wife.' He said, 'Well, I wouldn't do that yet. She doesn't know about this.' So that's Ernie Banks."

Don Kessinger, who lay claim to the shortstop position in the same infield as Banks and Beckert, said there is no question about it, what Beckert said about Banks being a talkaholic is true.

"Oh, Ernie just had a great time," Kessinger said. "You came to the ballpark every single day and he said, 'It's a great day for baseball. It's a Cubs day. We're gonna get 'em today.' I mean, it was the same thing every day. And out on the field he's at first base and he might yell over to me at shortstop, 'Hey, Kess, how you doing?' I mean, he just carried on all the time. You say chatter to baseball people and they're talking about, 'Hey, let's go,' or whatever that stuff is. I mean, he just carried on about everything. He just had a good time. He loved being at the ballpark.

"I love Ernie Banks. It's just hard to carry on a conversation with him sometimes."

The Cubs of the 1960s were a special group. The players were close, had fun together, and had some stretches where they won a lot of games.

"That was a good group," Banks said.

Third baseman Ron Santo, another All-Star, rocked the house at Wrigley when he began clicking his heels together after a victory. That tickled Banks.

"That was wonderful," Banks said. "The other team didn't like it, but we didn't have to count on those guys liking it. At Wrigley Field, we have our own world there. The Cubs are a special franchise and we have our own world. The park, televising all of the home games, and cable TV."

Banks said P. K. Wrigley was visionary for televising home games, not just locally, but through the use of the WGN superstation nationally.

"Somebody was telling Mr. Wrigley that by televising all of his home games it would decrease the fan base," Banks said. "And he said, 'No, I'm generating fans, bringing other people out to watch the game. When school's out and later on they become fans.' That's the truth.

"The unusual thing about the Cubs is that it is a generational team. The fathers come, the grandfathers come, the children, the grandchildren. That's a wonderful dynamic to me. There's no other professional team like that. None at all. There are fans coming out now, their fathers came, their mothers came, their grandparents came. It's perpetuated. It gets bigger and bigger and we need more seats there. Because more people want to come.

"Wrigley Field's about love. It's sitting close to each other. When somebody goes to the concession stand, they can bring you a Coke back. They can bring you a hot dog back. It's just friendly people. It's a wonderful place. And the players are that way, too. The Cubs players historically are the nicest people I've ever been around. They're really nice guys."

Banks lives in California, but attends games at Wrigley each summer and makes a point of being in attendance for special occasions, such as the 2005 retirement of second baseman Ryne Sandberg's No. 23. There's no doubt Banks feels the love when he makes return engagements. It is impossible to imagine the Wrigley crowd not embracing him wildly.

"It is amazing, phenomenal," Banks said of his appearances. "All of us, Ronnie Santo, Billy Williams, Fergie, all of us just love the people. A lot of them there now, their fathers saw me play, so they kind of passed the information on to the kids and the kids follow us. It's different than any other place. It really is."

Just listening to Banks rhapsodize about the fans and the Wrigley Field of today offers a glimpse into what it was like being around him for a long season.

"Ernie was always cheerful," said pitcher Ferguson Jenkins, one of the greatest throwers in Cubs history. "He was always bubbly, always wanting to talk to the fans. I roomed with Ernie for a while at the end of his career. I just think that when you have players who enjoy what they do for a living, they're happy all the time, and Ernie was that type of individual."

Player Joe Amalfitano once said, "When Ernie dies and the undertaker gets through with him, he'll look up and say, 'Nice job, buddy.'"

Banks, of course, might have been the team leader in laughter, but he also led the Cubs in more empirical hitting categories.

"Ernie did what he could do to win ballgames on a daily basis," Jenkins said. "He was in the lineup every day playing first base and he was one of our leaders."

The Cubs did not wait until the end of Banks' playing days to honor him. At the height of his career, August 15, 1963, was proclaimed "Ernie Banks Day." Mayor Richard J. Daley proclaimed it Banks Day in the community, as well. During a 22-minute ceremony, Banks was presented with an air-conditioned, nine-passenger station wagon, a diamond ring, a transistor radio, savings bonds for his three kids, a sterling silver tray, and a hi-fi player.

"First of all," Banks said during the event, "I want to thank God for making me an American and giving me the ability to be a major league player. I will be forever grateful. Everything I have I owe to baseball."

Banks' image transcended Chicago. If you were a baseball fan and you read about the game, listened on the radio, and watched the game of the week or the All-Star Game, sooner or later an analyst would talk about Banks. Santo, one of Banks' long-time infield partners, said he thought highly of Banks before he ever met him.

"It was just the way he hit and the way he conducted himself," Santo said. "I enjoyed the way he wiggled his fingers before hitting a baseball, hitting line drives, and he was so quick."

Santo came to the majors in 1960 at a time when rookies were meant to be seen and not heard. The veterans ran the clubhouse and often gave rookies the silent treatment, or in some cases resented their presence because they were taking a veteran's job on the roster.

Santo made his big-league debut at old Forbes Field in Pittsburgh. When he got to the park he had no idea he was playing, but manager Lou

DID YOU KNOW . . . That Ernie Banks held the top hitting marks for home runs and RBIs at first base and shortstop for more than 40 years until Derrek Lee broke his records at first base during the 2005 season?

Boudreau called him into the office and told him he was in the lineup and hitting sixth.

Dressed early, Santo went out and just sat in the visitors dugout, soaking up the atmosphere.

"As I'm sitting there before batting practice, Ernie Banks comes out and sits next to me," Santo recalled. "In those days nobody talked to you. Do you understand? You're a rookie and you've got to prove yourself because there were only 400 ballplayers in the majors and you're taking the job of one of their friends.

"Here comes Ernie and he sits right next to me and he says, 'Are you nervous, kid?' I said, 'Oh yeah, Ernie.' And he said, 'Well, look at these two guys [for a doubleheader].' Guess who was pitching? Vernon Law and Bob Friend. One was a 20-game winner and one was a 19-game winner. And Ernie says, 'Look at these two guys as if they are Triple A pitchers.' And I looked at Ernie and I said, 'That's easy for you to say.'"

More than three decades after his playing days ended, Banks thinks more about non-baseball topics. Making it into the Hall of Fame in 1977 was great, but Mr. Cub has grander aspirations these days. A man whose good intentions and big heart have never been questioned, would like to win the Nobel Prize for Peace.

Of course, someone must be officially nominated for consideration and that also means achievements must be recognized and appreciated. When Banks was asked what he hopes to nominated for, he said, "I'm still working on that idea. My field is to try to help eliminate poverty."

Certainly, that is a worthy goal, and anyone, politician, world leader, philanthropist, or sportsman, who not only annunciates the problem, but who could solve it, would deserve a Nobel Prize. Banks noted that many of today's richest athletes in major sports already have demonstrated the consciousness to help others by setting up foundations to give back to communities and to return some of their riches to those less fortunate.

"I've met some people who have foundations to help people who suffered," Banks said. "And I've met with a lot of athletes who deal with disadvantaged poor people. Tiger Woods, Michael Jordan, a lot of athletes. I'm going to try to round them up together so we can all join in as a team, link them all together."

That is the Ernie Banks plan to end world poverty in its embryonic stages. If he can link all of those headstrong athletes together, from baseball to football, from basketball to hockey, from boxing to golf, his old nickname of Mr. Cub might morph into something more all-encompassing. We'll be calling Banks Mr. Miracle Worker.

How Many College Graduates Does It Take to Make a College of Coaches?

It might be the battiest idea ever advanced by an owner. Forget colored baseballs, Charlie Finley. Forget managing the team by yourself, Ted Turner.

Baseball teams have always had a boss on the field, a field general, as they are sometimes called. And unlike other major sports, the dugout leader has always been called a "manager" rather than a "head coach."

So imagine the amazement, the skepticism, and the ridicule that spread through the sport like an out-of-control forest fire when on December 21, 1960, Cubs owner P. K. Wrigley announced his plan for the next season: a rotating team of managers. Almost immediately, members of the press, recognizing that too many managers was like having no manager at all, named the group the "College of Coaches." Others were tempted to call it the "circus." There had never been anything like it in major league baseball history, and there never would be again.

When he revealed the proposal, Wrigley said, "I don't believe any organization is dependent on one man. Look at the federal government. It is giving the vice president more responsibility. And commissions are being appointed all over the place."

It was clear that Wrigley was not looking for strong leadership, but more like caretakers to run the club.

"Heavens," he said, "we don't need a dictator."

Fans and former players heckled the idea almost as loudly as sportswriters. Fred Lindstrom, the Hall of Fame infielder, pretty much stated that Wrigley didn't know what he was talking about.

"It is most apparent from his remarks about baseball managers that Mr. Philip K. Wrigley of the Chicago Cubs has never been exposed to the

TOP TEN

Cubs Single-Season Wins for Pitchers

	Name	Year	Wins
1.	Mordecai "Three Finger" Brown	1908	29
2.	Mordecai "Three Finger" Brown	1909	27†
	Grover Alexander	1920	27†
4.	Mordecai "Three Finger" Brown	1906	26†
	Larry Cheney	1912	26†
	Charlie Root	1927	26†
7.	Mordecai "Three Finger" Brown	1910	25
8.	Ed Reulbach	1908	24†
	Larry Jackson	1964	24†
	Ferguson Jenkins	1971	24†

value of a truly great leader like John McGraw and his dynamic personality," Lindstrom said.

It was not most apparent just what Wrigley was looking for—except for a fresh way to try to win. By 1960 winning had become almost a foreign concept for the Cubs. Fifteen years had passed since Chicago's last National League pennant. Wrigley also made one key point that no one could argue with.

"We certainly cannot do much worse trying a new system than we have done for many years under the old," Wrigley said.

A visionary plan? Or a crackpot idea?

Coaching roulette began in 1961. Wrigley hired 11 men to fill out the staff. At any given time, some were roving through the minor leagues, some were in the major league dugout, and one was in charge. However, the pseudo-manager was generally in charge for only a few weeks at a time.

The group of coaches who gave the operation a go that season included good old Charlie Grimm, who was ultimately hired as Cubs manager by Wrigley four times (George Steinbrenner had nothing on Wrigley when he played musical chairs with Billy Martin years later). Besides Grimm, Harry Craft, Bobby Adams, Elvin Tappe, Lou Klein, Dick

Cole, Rip Collins, Vedie Himsl, Gordie Holt, Fred Martin, and Verlon Walker constituted the braintrust.

It is priceless to picture the staff meetings. Were 11 heads really better than one? They might have been if they didn't have different thoughts in mind about how to hit the curveball. Tappe, Himsl, Craft, and Klein took turns as head coach during the summer. It was suggested by some that there was behind-the-scenes backstabbing between coaches who aspired to take over. It was also felt that some players tended to ignore suggestions from one coach while waiting it out until the next coach took over.

Long-time third baseman Ron Santo had just broken into the majors as a 20-year-old and was starting his second season when the College of Coaches was instituted. Santo remembers it well, but didn't know what to make of the situation.

"I can't even remember if they were going to switch every two weeks or one week," said Santo, now a Cubs broadcaster. "You had a head coach and he was supposed to be your manager, but he was a coach. Then each one of them who took over had his own ideas about how to play the game.

"And the next guy was different. It could be confusing. Fortunately, I was able to give myself a pat on the back because I knew I had God-given ability making the big leagues at 20 years old after just one year in the minor leagues. I knew I was going to stay in the big leagues. I had a gift, but sometimes you want to get some experience from your coaches and manager. But I had to let some things go in one ear and out the other. In other words, I would nod 'Yes' and I would do what I thought was good for me. It was just way too much overload."

The system was bucking nearly a century's worth of tradition. Part of that ingrained pattern was recognizing the manager as king and the coaches more as buddies whom you could talk with a little bit more.

"You really had respect for managers," Santo said. "A coach, if you got upset at him [though not at my age] you could say, 'Bullshit.' But with a

TRIVIA

Which Cubs pitcher had the lowest single-season earned-run average in team history?

Answers to the trivia questions are on pages 158–159.

IF ONLY . . . There had been one Einstein among the 11 coaches in the Cubs' College of Coaches, the team might have made history and introduced a new model for operating professional franchises. Instead, the lost seasons of 1961 and 1962 merely followed the team's pattern of losing often and big during the bad old days.

manager, you couldn't do that. So here you were getting coaches every two weeks, or whatever it was, and they're trying to win ballgames, so that maybe at the end of the year they would become the head guy."

The College of Coaches did not seem to possess the combined know-how of the College of Musical Knowledge and did not produce results any more exciting than, as Wrigley would have it, a dictator. The team finished 64–90 during the 1961 season, in seventh place, 29 games out of first.

Grimm, the former player who had managed and done broadcast work, found himself back in the mix. Jolly Cholly joked about his return to uniform with famed sportswriter Red Smith.

"Treadmill to nowhere, eh?" Grimm said. "And here we go again. It's all sort of a surprise to me."

Cubs Hall of Famer Ernie Banks, who had suffered through some frustrating campaigns while winning two Most Valuable Player awards for losing teams, at first embraced the College of Coaches.

"It was great," Banks said. "If a younger player in the minor leagues came up to the Cubs, they knew the person that was the manager. Everybody knew each other."

By blessing the ill-fated College of Coaches, Banks at the least lives up to his reputation as a nice man who has never said a bad word about anybody.

"I think Mr. Wrigley was a pathfinder," Banks said. "A visionary. He was a little before his time."

Maybe so, but in the four-plus decades since, no one else has been tempted to scrap the manager's job for a team approach running a major league ballclub.

The Cubs were actually worse in 1962, the second year of the College of Coaches experiment. They finished 59–103 and 42½ games out of first. That placed them ninth in the expanded league. There were

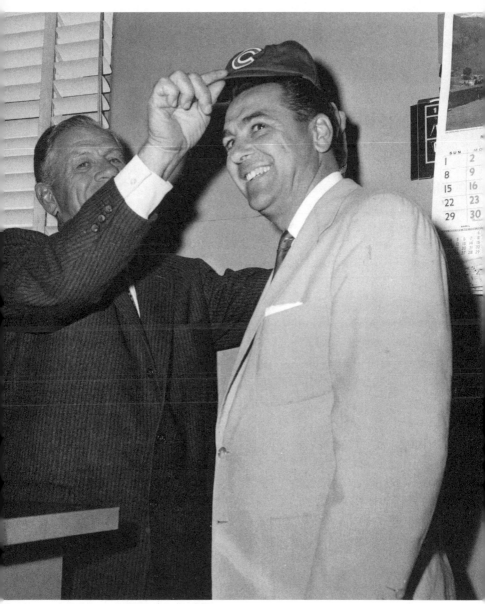

Charlie Grimm (left), who spent a half century as a Cubs player, coach, manager, and broadcaster, crowns Lou Boudreau with a Cubs cap. The two traded jobs, with Grimm moving from the dugout to the radio booth and Boudreau taking over as manager.

fewer temporary managers that season. Tappe was 4–16. Lou Klein 12–18 and Charlie Metro ran the show the rest of the season.

Banks did not enjoy the losing.

"It was a horror," Banks said. "Metro was talking to somebody and said, 'Boy, the way these guys are playing, I'd like to come out here with my 30.06.'"

Metro never did turn a weapon on his players out of frustration, but after baseball, Banks said Metro went off to the Colorado mountains to raise horses. He probably did not share the foreman's responsibility on his ranch with 10 others.

Tappe, said Banks, is the one who suggested the aging Banks shift from shortstop to first base.

"He called me up in my hotel room and asked, 'You got a first baseman's glove?' I said, 'No.' He said, 'Well, you're gonna play first base tomorrow night in San Francisco.'"

And that's where Banks stayed and played in the latter stages of his career.

No matter what the Cubs tried and no matter who delivered the lineup card to home plate, the losing never stopped under the College of Coaches.

"We were losing so much that everybody was doing a little panicking," Banks said. "All of the coaches were a little panicky. They all wanted to be the head coach who brought us out of the slump. All we did was just the best we could to try to get out of the slump."

Only they never did.

By 1963 the lines of authority had been spelled out. Bob Kennedy still bore the job title of head coach, but he was the only head coach. Nobody else rotated into the top slot. Wrigley was infatuated with the word "coach" apparently and clung to it, but Kennedy—by himself—led the Cubs to an 82–80 record that season.

Kennedy was manager in all but name, but when no-nonsense Leo "the Lip" Durocher took over for the 1966 season he made certain to clarify his stance instantly. Durocher was the manager. Period.

Of course, Durocher also proved he was no Jeanne Dixon when it came to predicting the future. And even if he thought he was a guy who was never wrong, with a crystal ball shinier than Dixon's, his lip did lead him down erroneous paths.

Durocher was hired because the Cubs finished 72–90 in 1965, the eighth place team in the National League. Famously, at his meet-and-greet press conference, Durocher, at high decibel level, proclaimed, "This is no eighth-place club."

He was correct in a way he had not anticipated. The Cubs won only 59 of 162 games that season and finished not eighth, but 10th in the standings.

The College of Coaches received a failing grade, but Durocher, despite his shaky start, was ushering in better times for antsy Cubs fans who had gone a full generation since appearing in the 1945 World Series.

A Cub for Life

Every so often a player becomes identified with a team so closely that mention of his name is the same as simultaneously mentioning the name of the team.

Ernie Banks is known around the country as Mr. Cub for his Hall of Fame career, but Ron Santo is known in Chicago as the guy who truly bleeds for the Cubs. Santo, a should-be Hall of Fame third baseman, is one guy who still thinks "we" when he talks Cubs baseball.

In a way, Santo stepped onto third base for the Cubs in 1960 and never left. He is as much of a fixture at Wrigley Field as the ivy. He is as rooted in Cubs lore as daytime baseball. He is as connected to the Cubs as the Wrigley family and current owners the Tribune Company.

Santo, who turned 65 before the 2005 season, came out of Seattle to join the Cubs in 1960 and occupied the third base bag through 1973. In 2005 he completed his 15th year as a WGN radio analyst, and if anyone listens to his broadcasts they know which side he is on. Santo takes defeat harder than some of the players. He is very much the partisan fans' commentator.

As a player, Santo was one of the best of his generation. He won five Gold Glove awards for his fielding prowess, was selected to play on nine All-Star teams during a 15-season career, and retired with a .277 batting average and 342 home runs, 337 as a Cub.

"He should be in the Hall of Fame," said Hall of Fame baseball writer Jerome Holtzman, who covered Santo's playing career.

Santo reached the majors as a 20-year-old. But he had such a belief in his talent and was so anxious, that timetable seemed slow for him. He played one year of Double A ball in the minors and then was invited to Cubs spring training in Mesa, Arizona, as a non-roster player.

By the NUMBERS 16—The number of consecutive seasons the Cubs and their fans endured without finishing over .500, from 1947 through 1962.

Third base (as it has been so often since Santo's retirement) was wide open for the taking in 1960. Santo was a spring phenom, turning heads, making coaches and players wonder who that newcomer was. As spring training was winding up, Santo said manager Charlie Grimm told him if he had a good weekend in an upcoming series against the Los Angeles Dodgers, "You're gonna be my third baseman." Santo played well in that series, and Grimm told him to move into the team hotel.

Excited, Santo thought he had it made. And then, just before camp broke, the Cubs traded for Don Zimmer, and team officials told him they thought he was too young to claim the job. Santo was infuriated. He exploded at Grimm.

"You lied to me, Charlie," Santo said. "That's baloney. You told me I was the third baseman. I know I can play in the big leagues. I don't like to be lied to."

Santo walked out of Grimm's office feeling betrayed and told himself, "I quit." He called his wife and told her he was coming home.

However, General Manager John Holland sought out Santo and attempted to soothe him. He knocked on the door of Santo's hotel room and Santo immediately said, "I'm going home. He lied to me. I know I can stay in the big leagues."

Holland understood the kid had a lot of potential and he certainly didn't want to lose him over this flap, so he played out a role that is probably best described as part fatherly and part sympathetic boss.

"It was, 'Come on, Ron, you don't want to leave. Blah, blah, blah,'" Santo said. "He said, 'I'll give you a major league contract to play Triple A ball.' I said, 'It's not the contract.' But he talked me into it."

A few months later, Zimmer, who much later would manage the Cubs in one of their favorite post–World War II seasons, was gone. Lou Boudreau, the Hall of Fame shortstop with the Cleveland Indians who was then a Cubs broadcaster, was interviewing Zimmer. They got to talking about the College of Coaches and Zimmer spoke candidly.

"This coaching system isn't worth anything," Zimmer said. "It's going to ruin two young guys."

He singled out Santo and young star outfielder Billy Williams. After the 1961 season, Zimmer was sent to the New York Mets. But well before that Santo had replaced him at third anyway, with Zimmer moving to second base. Santo made his major league debut on June 26, 1960, in a doubleheader against the Pirates. The Cubs won 7–6 and 7–5, and Santo was a major contributor. He swatted three hits and had five RBIs.

However, before the game, Santo concedes to being a nervous wreck. Santo had never set foot in a big league ballpark, and Forbes

Young Ron Santo, the best National League third baseman during his playing days, takes a throw for a putout. Santo was a team leader and top fielder and hitter from 1960 to 1973, and later returned to the team as a broadcaster.
Photo courtesy of National Baseball Hall of Fame Library, Cooperstown, New York.

Field was the first. He watched Pirates greats Roberto Clemente, Dick Groat, and Bill Mazeroski warm up and then he went back into the visitors' clubhouse. That season Boudreau and Grimm swapped jobs, with Grimm moving to the radio booth and Boudreau moving down to the field. It was Boudreau who inserted Santo into the starting lineup and told him he was batting sixth.

Ernie Banks tried to calm Santo by indicating the Pirates' stars (who would win the World Series that year) were just regular guys. Still, when Santo took batting practice, his nerves prevented him from hitting a ball out of the cage.

Bob Friend was the Pirates' starter, and his first pitch to Santo was a curveball that broke so sharply, Santo said his knees buckled. Catcher Smoky Burgess returned the ball to the mound and said, "That's a major league curve, kid." Santo said he stepped back into the batter's box, "and I hit a line drive up the middle for a base hit."

Undeniably, Santo had talent and aptitude and was going to make it big in baseball. He had been successful at the local level in Seattle and was heavily pursued by many big league clubs. In the 1950s teams employed squadrons of keen-eyed scouts with savvy judgment to ferret out talent everywhere and anywhere. There was no universal draft. It was each team for itself.

In the baseball world of 1959, Seattle was more backwater than big league, but the scouts found Santo, and after he completed high school, they lined up at his home to make offers.

"I had all 16 major league teams after me," Santo said, "and they came one at a time. The Cleveland Indians were the first team I saw. They offered me—this is amazing in 1959—$50,000 to sign. I lived in a duplex, and I had my stepfather John Constantino and my mother, and we didn't have a lot of material goods. I couldn't even swallow when I heard it."

Dave Kosher, a bird-dog scout for the Cubs, had been the first to notice Santo as a sophomore. Kosher, whose health problems kept him in a wheelchair and caused him to slur his words, was the first to tell Santo he would be a big leaguer. The prediction shocked Santo. Santo made an all-star team representing Washington state and traveled to New York. At the time he was a catcher because of another player's injury, but he loved third base.

TOP TEN

Oldest Major League Ballparks

	Ballpark	City	Date Opened
1.	Fenway Park	Boston	April 20, 1912
2.	Wrigley Field	Chicago	April 23, 1914
3.	Yankee Stadium	New York	April 18, 1923
4.	Robert F. Kennedy	Washington	April 9, 1962
5.	Dodger Stadium	Los Angeles	April 10, 1962
6.	Shea Stadium	New York	April 17, 1964
7.	Angel Stadium	Anaheim	April 19, 1966
8.	Network Associates Coliseum	Oakland	April 17, 1968
9.	Kaufman Stadium	Kansas City	April 10, 1973
10.	Hubert H. Humphrey Metrodome	Minneapolis	April 6, 1982

Santo recalled what happened afterward: "After that all-star game, Dave said, 'You know, I'm going to be coming to see you because we're very interested in you.' I said, 'Oh, great.' Then I hear from the other 15 teams, and no offer was less than $50,000. In fact, the Cincinnati Reds were in the $80,000s and the Yankees were up at $75,000 or something. And I don't hear from Dave."

At last, after all of the other teams paraded through the Santo home, Kosher called.

"It was almost like he was crying," Santo said. "And he said, 'Ron, I know what you've been offered and we can't even come close to that. All they're gonna offer you is $20,000.'"

Santo told Kosher he still hadn't made up his mind and to come over with head scout Hard Rock Johnson. Johnson made the $20,000 offer and said the Cubs wanted Santo to catch. Santo said his stepfather could barely contain himself, thanked Johnson, and cut short his presentation. Johnson left, but Santo urged Kosher to stay.

Santo drove Kosher home and told him he hadn't made up his mind. Later that night Santo discussed the offers with his stepfather and said he was entranced by the idea of playing in Wrigley Field and that the money didn't mean as much as the chance to play in the big leagues. Santo signed with the Cubs.

"I went to a three-week camp in Arizona with all the top rookies," he said. "I'm a catcher and I had three real good weeks. They invited me to stay with the big league club. I was the last cut and I was sent to Double A ball. I spent one year in Double A ball and two months in Triple A, and I was in the big leagues. So I made up the difference in money."

The one thing that could potentially disrupt Santo's dream of playing Major League baseball was a diagnosis at age 18 that he had juvenile diabetes and would have to inject himself with insulin for the rest of his life. Confused after being told he had a disease that he had no knowledge of and that could some day kill him, Santo was at first in denial.

Over time, as Santo explained in his 1993 autobiography *Ron Santo: For Love of Ivy*, written with Randy Minkoff, he came to understand how the illness could affect his kidneys, eyesight, circulation, and other functions. But he chose a policy of secrecy among his teammates. He didn't want the Cubs to know about his diabetes; he didn't want any taunting by opponents, and he didn't want any coach or manager to hold it against him when passing judgment on his play.

Much later, Santo was the road roommate of second baseman Glenn Beckert, who discovered Santo's secret. Beckert tells the story on himself to demonstrate his own naïveté and ignorance about the disease then.

The Cubs were on a road trip to San Francisco to play the Giants, and at the time Santo was on a tear, batting something like .336. Beckert, meanwhile, was in a slump, hitting about .211.

"One morning I saw him give himself an injection in the bathroom," Beckert said of witnessing Santo's insulin shot. "And I said, 'Whoa, rooms, we've gotta talk about this one. This is serious stuff here. You know you're hitting .336. What are those medications you're taking? I need some of that.'

"So that was funny. He had kept it very quiet that he was a diabetic."

Later in life Santo has been deeply affected by his struggle with diabetes. He has had parts of both legs amputated because of the disease and has

TRIVIA

Who preceded Dusty Baker as manager of the Cubs?

Answers to the trivia questions are on pages 158–159.

also had to fight cancer. None of the health problems kept him out of the broadcast booth and away from Wrigley Field and the Cubs for long. Also, in contrast to his initial inclination to hide his affliction, Santo became a very public fighter seeking to help researchers find a cure. A board member of the Juvenile Diabetes Research Foundation, he has organized a Ron Santo Walk for the Cure for more than a quarter century. The 2003 walk alone raised $5 million for diabetes research.

Santo enjoyed a marvelous baseball career, enjoys every minute of his broadcast time (including mishaps like getting his hair piece caught in a fan in the booth and once setting himself on fire during a broadcast), but has also inspired Chicagoans with his courage coping with ill health.

Santo's son Jeff, a film director, made an inspiring documentary about his father that highlighted Santo's struggles and spirit, culminating with the retirement of his No. 10 jersey by the Cubs during the 2003 season. It is called *This Old Cub* and was released in 2004. Santo at first resisted some of the filming for privacy reasons and was not sure anyone would be interested. However, the film is moving, tasteful, and is clearly done lovingly despite Jeff Santo's attempts at detachment.

More recently, Santo has penned another book with New York sportswriter Phil Pepe called *Few and Chosen*. Naturally, it is about the Cubs. Although the book pretty much presents what it means to be a true Cub, surprisingly, Santo said he doesn't think about that very much.

"I've always been a Cub," he said. "I can't tell you what it means. A lot of people will say to you, 'How can you be such a Cub when you haven't won in 90-something years? How could you?' I said when I retired that there was no team I would give up my 14 years as a Cub for a World Series with anybody else."

And here is Santo, still a Cub.

"And always will be a Cub," he said. "I would not, if I had the opportunity, would never go into broadcasting for anybody else. When I started broadcasting, I didn't think it was for me. I thought I was embarrassing myself, but the general manager said to me, 'Let me hear a tape.'

And then he said, 'That's you, Ron, and we want you to be you.' From that moment on I've been me."

That's why Cubs fans love Santo's commentary as much as they loved him as a player.

"Whatever the moaning and groaning I do, and I don't even realize I'm doing it, I'd be doing it at home," Santo said.

Just like all of those other true-blue Cubs fans.

The 1960s Soap Opera

The short and bitter saga of Ken Hubbs' stay with the Cubs might well have made intense fans think the club was cursed beyond the issue of advancing to the World Series.

Hubbs was a phenom who at age 20 burst into the lineup as a second baseman of supreme excellence in 1962. Hubbs set a then-record of errorless play at the position for 78 games, batted .260, and was a near-unanimous Rookie of the Year.

He was clearly a star in the making and, with Santo at third, seemed likely to anchor the Cubs' infield for years. A spectacular play at the end of the 1962 season solidified the impression that Hubbs would only improve. He was the focal point of a triple play.

On September 30, as the Cubs bested the Mets at Wrigley Field for the New Yorkers' still-standing single-season record 120th loss, the Cubs achieved the three outs on one play in the eighth inning. Hubbs started it all. Hubbs chased down a short pop into right field with his back to the plate, retiring batter Joe Pignatano, then spun and fired a throw to Ernie Banks covering first base. That doubled up runner Richie Ashburn. Then Banks threw back to second for the putout on runner Solly Drake for the third out. An electrifying play.

And then all of the promise Hubbs had shown with his great instincts and winning personality evaporated. On February 13, 1964, Hubbs was piloting a single-engine Cessna 172 that he bought when he began flying lessons several months before. Flying near Provo, Utah, with his best friend, Dennis Doyle, Hubbs took off in a snow-storm with limited visibility and crashed five miles out of town. The accident killed both men. It might also have killed the Cubs' spirit for some time.

The first half of the 1960s was regarded as among the most tumultuous of times in American history. It included the hair-breadth of a difference in the presidential election between Richard Nixon and John F. Kennedy, Kennedy's November 1963 assassination, the escalation of the Vietnam War and the stirrings of the Civil Rights Movement. For the Cubs, the time period encapsulated a bizarre series of events extending beyond the experiment with the College of Coaches and the rise and tragic fall of Hubbs.

Ken Hubbs, 1962 Rookie of the Year who set fielding records at second base, seemed set for a long stay in the Cubs' infield, but had his career cut short by a tragic plane crash in a snowstorm that also killed his best friend.

51—During the 2000 season, the Cubs used a team-record 51 players in the field.

In another kooky move, owner P. K. Wrigley hired Robert Whitlow as athletics director. Athletics director? This was not the University of Cubs. Before 1964 and after 1965 the job of athletics director was solely identified with high school and college sports, not professional teams. Only the Cubs are the exception to the rule.

Whitlow was a retired Air Force colonel who had been athletics director at the Air Force Academy in Colorado Springs, Colorado. Unfortunately, he admitted he had seen only four or five major league games, so his baseball credibility was nil. And although the hire seemed like an off-the-wall idea and Whitlow seemed poorly equipped to handle it, the basic premise was sound. Wrigley wanted Whitlow to develop a more sophisticated conditioning and dietary program for his team and possibly to use computers to identify trends in the game.

Those suggestions have evolved into the norm in professional sports, but were deemed far out in the '60s. It's not clear even if a hard-nosed baseball man like Leo Durocher would have been able to push through those programs 40 years ago.

"We sure did do a lot of calisthenics," remembered Banks years later.

Then they went back to being baseball players.

Although it is little talked about today, unlike Jackie Robinson's breaking of the color line for players and Frank Robinson's distinction of becoming baseball's first black manager, in 1962 the Cubs hired Buck O'Neil as a coach.

O'Neil, a one-time star player and then manager in the Negro Leagues, and later renowned for his appearance in the Ken Burns *Baseball* documentary, became a scout for the Cubs in 1955. His ascension to coach, even though he split time between the Cubs and the club's minor league affiliates, made him the first black coach in major league history.

O'Neil made a simple statement when he was hired.

"I am very happy to have this opportunity of being a coach," he said. "I will do everything I can in helping the team's young ballplayers."

O'Neil remained a coach with the Cubs until 1965. He is now chairman of the board of directors of the Negro Leagues Museum in Kansas City.

There were some bad days for the Cubs in the early '60s, and nothing illustrated that more than the period near the end of the 1962 season, when it appeared even the most devoted fans had given up. On September 26 only 903 fans watched the Cubs lose to the Phillies. On September 28 only 595 fans watched the Cubs beat the Mets. During a 103-loss season (still 17 games better than the Mets!) the Cubs drew only 609,802. That was the worst attendance in the majors that year and in more than 40 seasons since, the Cubs have always drawn better.

If the Hubbs tragedy was sad in a purely human way, the defining baseball disaster of the period for the Cubs was the infamous trade of outfielder Lou Brock in June 1964. Mere mention of the future Hall of Famer in Chicago can still give a Cubs fan a headache, almost as if freezing cold ice cream has been downed too quickly.

Cubs fans are among the few sports supporters in the land who can nurse a hangover for more than four decades. The key protagonists in a six-player trade were Brock and pitcher Ernie Broglio. Fascinatingly, at the time Cubs fans thought they got the better of the deal. Brock was almost 25 and had hit only .257 with the Cubs. Broglio was 28 and coming off an 18–8 season.

Brock, of course, matured into a superstar who retired as baseball's since-surpassed leading stolen base thief. Broglio's arm fell apart and in parts of three seasons with the Cubs he was only 7–19. The swap is still regarded as one of the worst trades in baseball history.

Periodically, in the '60s the unthinkable was verbalized. Suggestions were made to trade an aging Ernie Banks. Charlie Metro, one of the rotating coaches, who actually made the vague comment "some people seem to be happier when we lose" about that system, thought trading Banks for valuable younger players would ensure the future success of the team.

That is one off-beat idea Wrigley never embraced, especially when such talk broke into the open again in 1966.

TRIVIA

Which two Cubs pitchers threw back-to-back one-hitters?

Answers to the trivia questions are on pages 158–159.

77

"Ernie started as a Cub and that's what he'll always be," Wrigley said. Pretty firm vote of confidence.

Bill Faul had a short career pitching for the Cubs in 1965 and 1966, but in his own way he was as memorable as the best players to wear the big *C* on their chests.

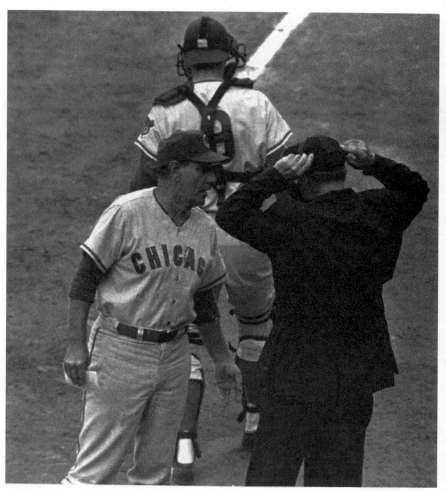

Mouthy Leo Durocher always spoke his mind, including on this occasion in 1966 in a game against the Braves, when he questioned umpire Shag Crawford's judgment. Durocher wanted nothing to do with the Cubs' experiment with a college of coaches and upon his appointment announced, "I am the manager."

THE 1960s SOAP OPERA

Faul, a one-time karate instructor, reportedly had his hands and feet registered with the police (or somewhere) as deadly weapons, something that sounded like a punchline on *Get Smart*, the spy sitcom of the era. In a rarity, he chose to wear uniform No. 13, but what gave him his greatest distinction was announcing that he was a master hypnotist who put himself into a trance before pitching.

Later, St. Louis Cardinals reliever Al Hrabosky stalked off the mound, pounded his glove, and performed a series of intense gyrations before facing batters. Genealogical researchers are still trying to determine if they are related. Faul also left the mound and kept his back to the batter and catcher. He waved his hand in front of his face—the supposed triggering mechanism for his concentration—then went into the windup.

Whether Faul was serious or putting people on, whether he was a true believer, or a light-hearted flake, not much aided him getting hitters out. In all he only won seven games for the Cubs. Still, he had to be good for the gate.

Leo "I'm-the-Manager" Durocher was hired for the 1966 season, and although he hung out with show business people (hobnobbing with the likes of Bob Hope and Dean Martin) and married show business wives (Laraine Day), Durocher was dead serious about baseball. The one-time Gashouse Gang shortstop was 60 years old and made his fame as skipper of the Brooklyn Dodgers and New York Giants, but hadn't managed in a decade. He still meant business. He also knew the game, but in the end made few happy in Chicago.

"Leo was a great manager," said former Cubs second baseman Glenn Beckert. "He did a great job for the Wrigley people and the Cubs, but we had some good talent sitting on the bench. He should have had some of them come in and give the guys a break for a few days."

In a place where playing all day games supposedly meant sapping the players down the stretch, that was an important point.

Durocher was nicknamed "the Lip" for good reason. He was blunt and didn't care if feelings got hurt. After a few years at the helm, one long newspaper story about him, relying heavily on unnamed sources, concluded that Durocher was both deeply feared and mightily disliked in Chicago.

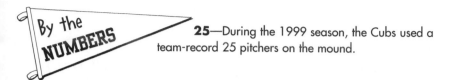

25—During the 1999 season, the Cubs used a team-record 25 pitchers on the mound.

One sportswriter called Durocher "a bully and a liar." Jerome Holtzman, the famous Chicago baseball writer, said that Durocher was jealous of Ernie Banks' stature in the town and treated him poorly. But Durocher was not brought to Chicago and the Cubs to make friends. He was brought to Chicago to win. In 1969 he was the leader of a team that for most of the season seemed destined to return the Cubs to the World Series for the first time in 24 years. But that came a little bit later, after he alienated many.

The Zillion-Dollar Infield

Too bad no one wrote a poem about them.

Or a song. Or maybe a short story. Or perhaps filmed a documentary. The wrong Chicago Cubs infield is immortalized. Tinker, Evers, and Chance did all right. But Banks, Beckert, Kessinger, and Santo was the all-time quartet guarding the four corners of the diamond. Ernie Banks, Hall of Famer and Mr. Cub in team lore, was at first base. Glenn Beckert was at second. Don Kessinger was at short. And Ron Santo was at third. At one time or another (and often the same time), all four were National League All-Stars.

"It was extremely good," said Jerome Holtzman, the Major League Baseball historian. "It was an all-star infield."

Banks' fame is enduring throughout the sport. Santo has been in the public eye, in Chicago, at least, for years. By comparison, Beckert and Kessinger, who spent nine years as the Keystone Cops protecting the middle of the infield, have more or less slipped from public attention.

Kessinger operates a real estate business in Oxford, Mississippi, one place where he is perhaps better known than Chicago. And Beckert lives in Englewood, Florida, on the western side of the state. Kessinger might appear in Chicago for an autograph signing once in a while, and Beckert might come north to sing "Take Me Out to the Ballgame" at Wrigley Field, but for the most part, they follow the Cubs from a distance now.

"We were both yesterday's news," Beckert joked after he and Kessinger appeared at a national sports collectors convention in the Chicago suburbs in 2005.

But in Chicago the news that the duo made, especially as part of the 1969 near-division-winner, is anything but. Fans remember the players, that team, and that era fondly.

By the
NUMBERS **164**—Both third baseman Ron Santo and outfielder Billy Williams played 164 games in what was originally a 162-game schedule during the 1965 season.

"It was a great infield," Kessinger said of his trio of partners. "The great thing was that we were able to play together for a long time, which doesn't happen in today's world so much. We were able to play together seven, eight, nine years. And we got to know each other. We knew what everybody did.

"Santo knew that if I went to my right with men on first and second with two outs I was probably coming to him with the ball. You just got to know those things about each other. We were all good friends, as well as good teammates, so that was a neat deal."

And yet they were only the second most famous infield in Cubs history.

"Well, maybe if we had gotten only about 12 double plays a year like Tinker, Evers, and Chance, we might have been [most famous]. Nope, there were no poems about us that I know of."

Kessinger, who starred at the University of Mississippi, made his Cubs debut in 1964 and stuck with the team until 1975. Beckert arrived in 1965, joining the threesome already in place and held his ground until 1973.

Kessinger played a team record 1,618 games at short, and Beckert played 1,206 games at second. Kessinger is the team career leader in assists with 5,346 for his position and in double plays with 982.

In 1969 Kessinger played 54 straight errorless games at short. Years later, he is not as lanky as he used to be, has less hair than he used to comb, and seems less impressed with his mark than ever.

"I think it's just one of those deals that—I mean this sincerely—it's just going out and playing," Kessinger said. "You know, it's just what I did. I played and I just did the best I could. As it got closer to the record, obviously I was aware of that and it probably was a little bit more pressure. But up until that time there really wasn't any. You were just going out and playing. When I got within seven, eight, or nine games of the record, obviously I started thinking about it a little bit."

Errorless streaks can be a funny thing. Some fielders don't have great range and don't reach the hard-to-play ball. Others get their hands on everything and can't possibly convert them all into outs. But for two months Kessinger had it both ways.

"I think you have to be really fortunate to go that many games without an error," he said. "You have to be fortunate because a ball can take a little bit of a hop at the last second that you're not expecting. It'll hit you on the wrist and honestly, if they hit that ball to you 100 times you'd probably miss it 99 out of 100. It's still an error. There's just nothing you can do about it.

Don Kessinger was one of the anchors of the Cubs' great infield of the late 1960s and early 1970s. The All-Star shortstop chased every ball and liked to measure his success by the number of assists he accumulated. Photo courtesy of National Baseball Hall of Fame Library, Cooperstown, New York.

"I really made more errors than others. I had a bad habit of really trying to throw everybody out if I thought I had any chance to get him. Sometimes you throw a ball away or you bounce one over there or something. Frankly, more than leading in percentage I was trying to get as many assists as I could. I thought if I could lead the league in assists or increase my assist number each year, then that's more people that I've gotten out. So my goal really was more to get the balls and try to make the plays and try to help the pitcher."

Beckert laughed as he described Kessinger's throws as they attempted the 4-6-3 double play, probably more casually decades later than he would have at the time.

"Sometimes," Beckert said, "it was Beckert to Kessinger to the first row of seats."

Beckert was a Pittsburgh guy, and Kessinger was a Mississippi guy. Their backgrounds were very different, but they became as close as brothers. Beckert said he was more earthy and used saltier language than Kessinger, who was a more religious southerner.

"I was a more outgoing person," Beckert said. "Don was very quiet, very religious. I can't mention some of the language I used. He was always very nice. His language...somebody would slide in hard and hit me or hit him and he was a gentleman. He'd say, 'Jiminy Cricket.' I was a Pittsburgh type, a blue collar type, similar to what [former Chicago Bears coach] Mike Ditka might say. Ditka played in our area. We played football, basketball, and baseball against each other."

Although Banks started out as a shortstop, he moved to first base in mid-career and slowed down in the field in his later years. Beckert said manager Leo Durocher didn't trust Banks' range in the late '60s, so he kept positioning Beckert farther and farther to his left, leaving a big hole in the center of the infield.

"I didn't have any great plays to the right," Beckert said. "But Kess had it both ways. We took it for granted that we knew what one another

IF ONLY . . . Players and teams stuck with each other longer, rather than making trades of stars in their prime, or in playing out their options so that the top players and fans could better cement their relationship.

DID YOU KNOW . . . That in 1968 Cubs third baseman Ron Santo and second baseman Glenn Beckert won National League Gold Gloves, and that in 1969 shortstop Don Kessinger won a Gold Glove at shortstop?

would do. I'm there, he's there, and it's automatic. Kess and I thought we would stay together forever. I was very fortunate because Don had great range. I had a little more trouble going to my right than to my left anyway."

Beckert was traded to the San Diego Padres later in his career, and if he didn't know how good he had it with Kessinger as a double-play partner, that was hammered home to him when he tried to adjust.

"It was very difficult for me after playing nine years with Kess," Beckert said, "and just knowing where each other was going to be."

There was a special closeness between the players who survived Leo Durocher's brusqueness, the transformation of the Cubs from losers to pennant contenders.

"Oh, it was remarkable," Kessinger said. "Playing with a group of guys who were all friends. We liked each other and got along as teammates. Beck and I got to know each other so well. No matter where the ball was hit, if it was a double-play situation, I knew exactly where Glenn Beckert was with the ball. Same way with Beck to me. There was just some intangible there."

Kessinger also got to know the fiery Durocher pretty well and he formed a mixed impression that pretty much mirrored history's view.

"I thought I learned more baseball under Leo than anybody else I was around," Kessinger said. "He really knew baseball, and the first two or three years he was in Chicago I learned a lot of baseball. But I thought Leo was a difficult guy to play for because he didn't believe in private meetings. He believed anything he had to say he could just say to the radio, the TV, the newspapers, or out in the clubhouse. He would second-guess a lot of guys on the field when he was in the dugout or he would criticize them."

Kessinger and Beckert marvel at how they have retained an enduring relationship with the team they played with for so long ago and how Wrigley Field, the ballpark they starred in, has become such a Chicago and American icon.

9—In 1929 the Cubs hit a team-record nine grand-slam home runs. Hack Wilson, Rogers Hornsby, and Charlie Grimm hit two each, and Riggs Stephenson, Kiki Cuyler, and Norman McMillan each hit one.

"I love the Cubs," Kessinger said more than 30 years after he left the team's infield. "I love Wrigley Field. I love everything about the organization. I think Wrigley's fame is partially because it has outlasted every place else. Everyone enjoyed coming to Chicago, and part of the thing we were known for then was all day games. Wrigley's always been a great place to play. Comiskey Park was still there. You had Tiger Stadium. Early on you had Forbes Field in Pittsburgh. There were a lot of older stadiums. Now there aren't, and Wrigley and Fenway Park kind of stand alone, or maybe Yankee Stadium to a degree, too.

"I was talking to a gentleman the other day, and he had gone to his first game at Wrigley Field. He actually was a Cardinals fan, but he had gone to watch the Cardinals and Cubs at Wrigley. I saw him at a little golf outing, and he came up to me and told me about it. He said it was the most unbelievable place. He said he had watched games on TV a number of times but couldn't really picture what it was like. He said—and I agree with this—that there's just ghosts out there. It's just a great place to watch a game. There's so much tradition."

The Cubs players and their fans develop a special bond, particularly if the players are long-time stars like Beckert and Kessinger. Maybe things were different when players made much less money and tended to stay with a team longer before the age of free agency.

"We liked the Cub fans," Kessinger said. "There was a relationship between the players with the fans...and fans to players, I don't even know how to explain it. But it was a great thing."

Kessinger and Beckert, whose heyday was 30 to 40 years ago, are forever identified as Cubs. They really feel they are Cubs for life.

"I think I am a great example of that," said Kessinger, who visits Chicago only a few times a year with his base in the Deep South. "The Cubs fans kind of adopted me, a little ol' country boy. I loved their fans and I think they loved me. It was a mutual deal. Not just me, the whole team. I mean, I left there and went to St. Louis for a year-and-a-half and then came back and I played with the White Sox and was a player/manager of the White Sox. But hardly anybody in Chicago realizes I was anything but a Cub.

"Yet in my three years with the White Sox, their fans treated me like a king. I was worried. So I have great respect for their fans, too. They treated Don Kessinger right at the end of his career. Chicago fans in general are just marvelous. I was a very fortunate person to have played for as many years as I did with the Cubs and in front of their fans in Wrigley Field, and then to get to come back and finish it up in Chicago. That was great, too."

For one, Beckert sounds just like a Cubs fan these days, as well. Cubs fans have been bereft of a World Series championship for nearly a century. The Cubs' last title came in 1908.

Glenn Beckert was Don Kessinger's second-base partner and Ron Santo's road roommate in a particularly tight-knit group of infielders, all of whom became All-Star performers. Photo courtesy of National Baseball Hall of Fame Library, Cooperstown, New York.

"I'd just love to see them win a World Series in my lifetime," Beckert said.

Heck, he has no grudges against the White Sox, either.

"The ultimate that could happen would be the White Sox against the Cubs in the World Series," Beckert said. "I don't know what you'd do in that town."

It would be one of the most joyous and tense Civil War series in all of sports.

A Nearly Perfect Season

It was the season that rekindled the fans' flame. It was the season that energized the Cubs for years. It was the season that was magical—until the spell wore off. But more than 35 years later, the 1969 season still means something special to long-time Cubs fans.

If nothing else, it will be remembered as the summer that Ken Holtzman pitched a no-hitter and Ron Santo clicked his heels together with the alacrity of dancer Gene Kelly.

By 1968 manager Leo Durocher had the Cubs playing good ball. The team finished 84–78 and in third place. There was some buzz in spring training in 1969. Was this the Cubs' year? It seemed like it when the club burst to an 11–1 start. It seemed like it when Ernie Banks, Glenn Beckert, Don Kessinger, Ron Santo, and catcher Randy Hundley—the entire infield—made the National League All-Star team. It seemed like it when the team set an attendance record of 1,674,993 fans (the record was 40 years old, and only three seasons earlier the Cubs drew a million fewer fans). And it seemed like it when the team won 92 games. Unfortunately, after leading the league most of the summer, a poor finish dropped the Cubs eight games behind the New York Mets. Outside of Chicago, that season is remembered as the year of the Miracle Mets, who won the World Series after fielding such dreadful teams earlier in the decade.

"I knew in spring training. I felt that year was going to be our year," Santo said. "I think everybody felt that way. We were a very close team. After a game we'd sit there and have a beer and talk for two hours before we'd leave."

Early in the season there was a peculiar incident played up in the newspapers. Owner P. K. Wrigley had gradually withdrawn from public view and never went to see his team play in person anymore. Suddenly, in April, there were hot rumors that Wrigley was seen observing in person the team that was off to a hot start.

Peanuts Lowrey, a coach with the Expos, said he saw Wrigley in the stands at an April 12 game. Ernie Banks said he saw him. The comments had a few days of life, and then General Manager John Holland put the kibosh on their veracity. The person in question in the box seats was Wrigley's cousin, who resembled him.

Randy Hundley, who pioneered the one-handed catching method perfected by Johnny Bench, is one player who will remember 1969 for other reasons. On May 27, his wife gave birth to a son, Todd, who later became a major league catcher, too, including a brief stint with the Cubs. The day after Todd Hundley was born, his dad hit a grand-slam homer.

After their fast start, the Cubs were in a mini-slump at the end of June before rallying to beat the Pirates 7–5 at Wrigley Field on Jim Hickman's two-run homer in the tenth inning.

"I got so excited when he came in I was pounding him on his head and then I ran down the left-field line, not even thinking, and just went up in the air and clicked my heels," Santo said. "I was so excited that we had maintained the lead."

It was not a premeditated gesture, and Santo thought little about the flamboyant maneuver until later that evening, when he was watching the news at home and video of him was aired running down the line and clicking his heels.

"I couldn't believe it," Santo said.

The next day at the park, Durocher called a team meeting and, standing in the middle of the clubhouse, he looked at Santo and said, "Ron, can you do that again?"

Santo was not sure he could replicate the move. But he figured the Bleacher Bums would urge him on and provide the adrenaline to perform.

"I said, 'What the heck,'" Santo said, "because you know I was that kind of guy. I was a very excitable guy. I did it just at home when we won and it became a thing that the fans would wait along the line as I ran down and clicked my heels three times. It was amazing. And then when I was driving home through the neighborhood, I had little kids running alongside my car and clicking their heels."

As might be expected in a professional sport where athletes hate to be shown up, other teams did not relish the performance. It angered

TOP TEN

Most Innings Pitched in a Single Season

	Name	Year	Innings
1.	Grover Cleveland Alexander	1920	363⅓
2.	Mordecai "Three Finger" Brown	1909	342⅔
3.	Jack Taylor	1902	333⅔
4.	Ferguson Jenkins	1971	325
5.	Ferguson Jenkins	1970	313
6.	Jack Taylor	1903	312⅓t
	Mordecai "Three Finger" Brown	1908	312⅓t
8.	Larry Cheney	1914	311⅓t
	Ferguson Jenkins	1969	311⅓t
10.	Charlie Root	1927	309

many and produced sarcastic comments, but Santo kept it up after each Wrigley victory.

"It was not done to show anybody up," Kessinger said. "That was such a spontaneous thing. If you listen to Ronnie do ballgames on the air now, he's enthusiastic. He loves the Cubs. It just happened one day. He just did it, not knowing everybody in the stands was going to see it and go crazy. It was for the fans and for us, his teammates."

As the Mets made their charge in the standings, they did not appreciate Santo's balletic leaps. After the Mets beat the Cubs in mid-July, Hall of Fame pitcher Tom Seaver darted out of the dugout and mocked Santo with his own heel click. But even now Kessinger has no sympathy for their attitude.

"Well, I mean, I'm sorry, but it's fun," Kessinger said. "It's crazy when you can't have a good time playing, isn't it?"

In August of 1968 southpaw Ken Holtzman's National Guard unit was activated for duty during the infamous rioting at the Democratic National Convention. A year later, on August 19, Holtzman pitched a no-hitter. He shut out the Atlanta Braves 3–0 and pulled off the trick without a strikeout. Holtzman, who won 174 big-league games, also shined with the early 1970s Oakland A's World Series teams.

Holtzman, who retired in 1979, became the physical education supervisor for a St. Louis–area Jewish community center and held the position for many years. He was never boastful about his no-hit day.

"I told everyone that pitching a no-hitter is strictly luck," Holtzman repeated in many forms over the years. "It's a well-pitched game with a lot more luck than usual."

Kessinger remembers the game well and took the opportunity to tease double-play partner Beckert, who scooped up a grounder and threw to first for the final out in the ninth inning.

"Last play of the game was a ground ball hit to Beckert at second base," Kessinger said. "And I thought he was going to stumble and fall.

"Everybody knew it was a no-hitter. Baseball's kind of superstitious. I don't recall there was a conscious effort not to say anything, but I would

Ken Holtzman, shown in 1969, when he pitched one of his two no-hitters in a Cubs uniform. The southpaw came out of the University of Illinois and was a key member of the rotation before moving on to World Series appearances with the Oakland A's. Photo courtesy of National Baseball Hall of Fame Library, Cooperstown, New York.

think, knowing baseball players, we probably didn't say anything. It's just kind of the way it is. Not that deep down I think it makes any difference whatsoever."

Still, the tension ratcheted up during the game and was quite tangible by the seventh inning.

TRIVIA

How many Cubs pitchers have won the Cy Young Award?

Answers to the trivia questions are on pages 158–159.

"Here's the deal," Kessinger said. "Even though it might not have been a perfect game [Holtzman walked three], if you make an error you haven't changed the fact that he has a no-hitter, but what you've done is give one more guy an opportunity to hit. You've given one more out to the other team."

As the summer of 1969 wore on, the Cubs created more and more excitement. By August 15, the Cubs were 30 games over .500, had an 8½-game lead over the second-place Cardinals, and were only dimly aware of the third-place Mets, 9-½ games behind.

Hall of Fame outfielder Billy Williams, another star on that Cubs club, maintains that it was a terrific team.

"It was a great infield," said Williams, who hit .293 with 103 runs scored and 95 RBIs that season. "They made the plays. You know, it's one of the greatest ballclubs ever to put on a uniform and perform that never won the World Series.

"We were going for it. We all thought this is our year to go to the World Series. We were loose. We were preparing for what would happen. Of course, it didn't happen, but it was one of the greatest summers I've ever enjoyed in Wrigley Field."

Williams still lives in the Chicago suburbs and makes many public appearances, so he is constantly reminded how much fans love the 1969 team.

"I go around and talk to them, and still a lot of people who are 45 and 50 years old say, 'That was the greatest summer of my life to come to Wrigley Field,'" Williams said.

It has often been suggested that the Cubs wilted many years because they played all home day games in the heat of the summer, while opponents played home games at night in cooler air. Beckert thinks the Cubs of 1969 did experience a loss of energy, and he thinks

9—Cubs Hall of Fame second baseman Ryne Sandberg won nine straight Gold Gloves for his exceptional play between the 1983 and 1991 seasons.

Durocher should have played more people off the bench instead of riding his stars full-time.

"Yes, I think the day games were a factor," Beckert said. "I think we ran out of gas. Leo should have given the guys a break. It all tied in together."

In fact, in one off-season, a newspaper story discussed Kessinger's slight build—a weight of only 166 pounds—and he told the writer from his home in Mississippi that he was constantly saying "pass the potatoes" at the dinner table in order to bulk up.

Despite 17 wins from Ken Holtzman, 20 from Bill Hands, and a 21–13 mark logged by Hall of Famer Ferguson Jenkins, who was in the midst of a run of six straight 20-victory seasons, the Cubs began their fade in mid-August, dousing their fans' spirits and their own. The Cubs fell out of first place after 155 days in the lead on September 10, and by September 15 the Cubs had lost 11 out of 12 games. The Mets, who won 38 of their last 49 games, clinched on September 24, then beat the Braves in the playoffs and the Baltimore Orioles in the World Series.

"I truly believe this," Kessinger said. "Had we won in 1969, we might have won two or three more times. But we didn't, so everybody focuses on 1969 as being the year the Cubs had a great team. I think we really were a great team from 1968 through 1972."

Octogenarian observer Jerome Holtzman agrees completely with Kessinger.

"They had the best team," he said. "I always felt if they had won it they would have won two or three more pennants in the next four years."

Instead, the Cubs did not have a similarly memorable season again until 1984, and halfway through the first decade of the 21st century, Jerome Holtzman was still forced to say, "They're gonna win. I don't know when."

Honors, but No Cigars or Champagne

No one has ever figured out why a pitcher can be magnificent one day and look ready to be exiled to the dog pound the next. Lefty Ken Holtzman, the author of a no-hitter in 1969, was carrying the statistical burden of a 2–6 record and a 5.40 earned-run average on June 3, 1971, when he took the mound against the Cincinnati Reds in Cincinnati.

On that day, Holtzman pitched a second no-hitter in a 1–0 victory, striking out six and retiring the final 11 men who came to bat. Later that night, sportswriter Jerome Holtzman, staying in the same hotel as the pitcher, had a phone call transferred to his room from the switchboard.

Minneapolis sportswriter Sid Hartman was on the other end of the line. He wanted an interview for a column to follow up on the no-hitter. He was looking for Ken Holtzman and hooked up with Jerome Holtzman, who on the spur of the moment decided to play a practical joke.

"I faked it and said I was Ken Holtzman," said Jerome Holtzman many years later. "I gave him a long interview. He didn't know it was me until a week later. He believed me."

Holtzman the pitcher was playing for the University of Illinois when the Cubs drafted him. After the Cubs selected him, General Manager John Holland stuck his head into the press box and asked Jerome Holtzman, "Do you have any relatives in St. Louis? We just signed a kid named Holtzman."

Jerome Holtzman said he had no idea who Ken Holtzman was. That would change.

"He was a pretty good pitcher," Jerome Holtzman said. "This Andy Pettitte, with Houston, he is a carbon copy of Kenny Holtzman, and no one ever mentions it."

By the NUMBERS

13—The Cubs had only 13 general managers between 1934 and 2005, with Charles Weber the first and Jim Hendry the most recent. John Holland (1957–1975) was the longest serving.

During the late 1960s and early 1970s, the Cubs had more than their share of pretty good players. Many stack up well with the best Cubs of all time.

Ernie Banks' 19-year career was winding down, but he was very much a revered figure in Chicago. In 1967, when the famed but controversial Picasso art piece was unveiled in downtown Chicago to much criticism, one alderman, John Hoellen, said the city got it all wrong. He labeled the sculpture "a rusting junk heap" and said it should be dismantled. Instead, Hoellen suggested, the city should erect a 50-foot statue of Banks because he is "the symbol of our vibrant city."

More than 35 years later, the Picasso sculpture remains in place, but Banks' reputation endures as well.

Banks' final major league game was the September 26, 1971, loss to the Phillies. Banks had a single that day. It was announced that Banks would stay with the Cubs as a coach. In accordance with P. K. Wrigley's observation as Banks being too nice a guy to manage and Banks' lack of interest in pursuing such a job, he never ran the team full-time. But on May 8, 1973, when manager Whitey Lockman was tossed from a game versus the San Diego Padres, Banks took over for the twelfth and last inning of a 3–2 victory. However brief the appearance was, Banks' fulfillment of the role made him the first black manager in baseball history.

Banks hit his 500th home run in 1970 and said the fastball that he powdered was inside and up. When the feat was recorded, he said he thought of his mother and father and Cubs fans and the organization.

The slugger finished with 512 homers and was renowned for repeating his motto, "Let's play two." It was representative of Banks' enthusiasm.

Banks was asked what kept him upbeat while playing on a losing team.

"We'd lose a ballgame and I'd get kind of down," Banks said. "But what the heck? When we lose, I start thinking about tomorrow. There's always tomorrow."

One of the Cubs' other great stars of the era was outfielder Billy Williams. When Williams played on September 2, 1970, he established a National League consecutive games streak of 1,117 straight games. The Dodgers' Steve Garvey eventually broke it, appearing in 1,207 straight games.

In 1972 right-hander Milt Pappas pitched one of the greatest games in Cubs history, though it has become famous nearly as much for what it almost was as compared to what it is.

The September 2 game was against the San Diego Padres, and Pappas retired the first 26 batters, putting him one out from a perfect game. In the ninth inning, Pappas went to 3-and-2 in the count against pinch-hitter Larry Stahl. The pitch that clinched the walk that ruined the perfect game was a very close pitch, but umpire Bruce Froemming called it a ball. Although Pappas got the following batter on a pop-up to record a no-hitter, he was furious. Over the years, Pappas showed no signs of mellowing. He thought he had struck out Stahl looking and that Froemming had stolen his perfect game with the wrong call.

"My fat buddy Bruce Froemming is still umpiring," Pappas said years later. "He's still ornery. Nobody likes the guy."

Wrigley Field maintained its image as a difficult place to pitch when the wind was blowing out. On April 17, 1976, the Philadelphia Phillies trailed the Cubs 13–2 after four innings, but won 18–16 in ten innings. In that game, Mike Schmidt, the Phillies' Hall of Fame third baseman, smashed a record-equaling four home runs.

While that performance was one for the record books, what happened barely more than a week later achieved societal distinction. On April 25 Cubs center fielder Rick Monday rescued an American flag from two miscreants who darted onto the field at Dodger Stadium in Los Angeles to set it ablaze on the 100th anniversary of the Cubs' first game.

IF ONLY . . . Young power hitter Andre Thornton and Manager Jim Marshall could have gotten along. Unfortunately, personality disagreements led to the trade of Thornton in his prime to Montreal for pitcher Steve Renko and outfielder Larry Biittner, neither of whom much helped the Cubs.

During the fourth inning, two fans climbed over the outfield wall and prepared to set the flag on fire. Monday ran over, scooped up the flag, and deposited it safely into the bullpen while the man and his son were arrested. Fans gave Monday a standing ovation, broke into a rendition of "God Bless America," and the Illinois State Legislature proclaimed a Rick Monday Day in order to honor his gesture. Nationwide, Monday was greeted as a hero. Monday's only lament was that the incident overshadowed his productive 19-year playing career. To this day, baseball fans who know Monday's name can't recount anything he did at bat or in the field but know him as "the guy who saved the flag."

A few years later, on May 17, 1979, the Cubs and Phillies competed in a slugfest that made their 18–16 show seem like a low-scoring game. This time the Phillies prevailed 23–22 in a game that featured 11 home runs, including three by the Cubs' Dave Kingman, and 50 hits. The 20-mph wind was naturally blowing out. It seemed you never knew when a typhoon might break out at Wrigley Field.

Marking the beginning of the end of a family era, P. K. Wrigley died on April 12, 1977, at age 82. The reclusive owner who rarely ventured to the ballpark in his last years was watching the Cubs on television when he passed away from a gastrointestinal hemorrhage at his Wisconsin home.

Somewhat fittingly, that was the year Banks was elected to the Hall of Fame on the first ballot. Wrigley lived to learn of Banks' honor, announced on January 19 (Banks telephoned him immediately) but not to see his enshrinement on August 8.

By far the biggest name in his Hall class, Banks could read an "America Loves Ernie Banks" banner at the induction ceremony. He praised Wrigley as a gentleman who gave him considerable confidence and, appropriately, Banks took note of the sunny day in Cooperstown, New York, and said, "There's sunshine, fresh air, and the team is behind us. Let's play two."

So Much More Than a Sidekick

Sometimes it seemed Billy Williams was an afterthought. Ernie Banks' slugging prowess and well-established reputation overshadowed the terrific accomplishments of the outfielder who is one of the greatest players in Cubs history.

Some sidekick. Williams, elected to the Hall of Fame in 1987, was the quiet hero of the Cubs during his career. He was not flamboyant and he was not outspoken. All he did was club home runs and drive in key runs year after year. Over 18 years, 16 of them with the Cubs, Williams averaged .290 at the plate, slugged 426 homers, and drove in 1,476 runs. He was Rookie of the Year in 1961 and won the 1972 National League batting championship.

At various times, Williams was called "Billy the Kid," was praised for his "great wrist action" and "level swing," and his "cool and calm attitude."

When Williams was being inducted into the Hall, Banks said, "I'm older than Billy, but he's my idol." It was the perfect compliment for a man who was durable and consistent for so long at Wrigley Field. Although Williams finished his career with the Oakland A's, he is forever a Cub. In the years after retirement as a player he was a Cubs coach and more recently has been a special assistant to the president. Williams is in frequent attendance at Wrigley and before games he often sits in the dugout observing batting practice and fielding warm-ups.

Williams grew up in Whistler, Alabama, and remains an avid fisherman, his childhood passion. He makes annual pilgrimages back home to see family and to fish in the same waters he knew as a youngster. Legendary coach Buck O'Neil discovered Williams' baseball talent.

Always trim and in perfect shape as a player, Williams is now graying, with a mix of white in his mustache, wears glasses, and is a little bit more heavyset around the middle.

The slugging left fielder made his major league debut in 1959, but had just cameo appearances until his breakout season of 1961 when he still qualified as a rookie. Despite his two-year sojourn in Oakland, Williams loved the old ways of day-time baseball with the Cubs and still identifies with the team that brought him up.

"One thing that attracted me at that time was playing all day games," Williams said while sitting in the empty Cubs dugout before a game during the summer of 2005. "It allowed me to spend time with the family and just enjoy Chicago and see what it was all about. You had Mondays and, possibly, Thursdays off."

Williams is another former player who appreciates the longevity of Wrigley Field. Although baseball is experiencing a surge of construction with new ballparks, Williams thinks the past is lost when a new ballpark cancels out an old park's memories.

"A lot of these kids won't know about things," Williams said. "They might have a manager who played in the old ballpark and he would point up and say, 'Why, Jimmy Wynn hit a home run here in the Astrodome' and a lot of these guys won't see it. The history of Wrigley Field is still there. Those guys who played in the past put a lot of history into Wrigley Field and Yankee Stadium and Fenway Park in Boston."

When Williams talks to Cubs newcomers these days, he not only recounts history, he primes them for what they are going to experience in the same park he played in, with the same type of exuberant fans.

TRIVIA

What is the largest number of players who made their major league debut in a Cubs uniform during a single season?

Answers to the trivia questions are on pages 158–159.

"You know, when you come to the ballpark and it's filled with people rooting for you, it gives you a good feeling," Williams said. "I tell a lot of them, 'You're in a great ballpark in a great city. Enjoy it while you're here because when you leave, it's going be a thing where you say, 'Man, that was great when I was in Chicago.'"

Outfielder Billy Williams was known for his sweet swing at the plate, and he put up Hall of Fame slugging numbers during his career. After retirement, Williams returned to the Cubs as a coach and currently serves as special assistant to the president of the team. Photo courtesy of National Baseball Hall of Fame Library, Cooperstown, New York.

TOP TEN

Cubs Leaders in Grand Slams

	Name	Grand Slams
1.	Ernie Banks	12
2.	Sammy Sosa	8†
	Bill Nicholson	8†
4.	Jody Davis	5†
	Gabby Hartnett	5†
	Andy Pafko	5†
	Ryne Sandberg	5†
	Ron Santo	5†
10.	Five players tied with 4	

The Cubs of the 1960s era were not only top-notch, they were particularly close. Banks, Williams, Ron Santo, Don Kessinger, Glenn Beckert, and Ferguson Jenkins all realized they had something special going. They socialized together, hung out in the clubhouse together, and in later years have been reunited at the annual January Cubs convention in Chicago, during the season at games, or annually at the Fantasy Baseball Camp organized by former catcher Randy Hundley. The others give credit to Hundley for rejuvenating their get-togethers as a group and say they love and are grateful for his efforts.

"That was a big factor in keeping everybody together," Williams said. "A lot of the guys enjoy those fans who supported us for so many years. They get a chance to rub shoulders, tell jokes, and enjoy being there. We have a lot of fun. It's like we're rewarding those guys for being so supportive over the years."

Back in their playing days, Williams said many of the key players' wives were friendly, too. And the players stayed in touch across the years.

"I was sitting watching a golf game the other day and Beckert called," Williams said. "I see Fergie. I see Santo out at the ballpark. We had a good time together and we still have a good time together."

Jenkins and Williams are still pals, too, when they overlap. Williams lives in the Chicago suburbs, and Jenkins lives in Arizona, but they do run into one another at games or events. Williams did many spectacular things with his bat, but Jenkins remembers additional qualities.

"Sweet-swinging Billy Williams," Jenkins said about his old friend. "Nobody had a better swing than Billy Williams. Believe me. Bar none, nobody had a better swing."

When people talked about Williams as an everyday player, they meant it. His record playing streak highlighted his routine appearance in all 162 games a season and sometimes more when ties were replayed.

"I mean, he was durable," Jenkins said. "Billy was always in the lineup. He was totally consistent. You loved the game, you came to the ballpark, you came to play, and that's what Billy did all of the time."

Williams roomed with Banks on the road and said the man was chattering all the time. Often it was fun to listen to Banks' stories, but other times Williams couldn't get any rest because Banks was a talking machine.

"I had to get out of that," Williams said. "I said, 'I've gotta get some rest.'"

Williams was a key player when the Cubs made their 1969 resurgence and began getting more popular, but not even he realized how many Cubs fans were sprinkled around the nation until he joined the A's and saw his former team in a different context.

"When I went back to the A's as a hitting coach in 1983, I would go to different major league cities and see people with Cubs memorabilia," Williams said. "They had on Cubs hats, Cubs jackets, and they would somehow venture down to the end of the stands and tell me how happy they were when the Cubs were winning."

Once Williams made a public speaking appearance with then-A's star Sal Bando in a town in California during the 1984 season.

"After we got through talking, this one individual came up to me and started talking, and tears were trickling down his cheeks," Williams said. "And he told me how happy he was that the Cubs were about to win the division title and possibly go on to be in the World Series. He said, 'My father waited for this a long time. He's not here, but I'm just elated. I'm really, really happy for the Cubs and I'm sorry he's not here to see this.' It was a big emotional moment for him."

Of course, the Cubs did not reach the World Series that year and Williams isn't going to take any Cubs advancement for granted before the game is officially placed into the win column.

"This is the game of baseball," he said. "You never know what's going to happen until the last man is out, you know. You could be going good, and all of a sudden things don't happen right for you. All of a sudden, you know, you're in a situation where you're gasping out there, but that's the game of baseball."

And don't the Cubs know that from experience.

The Man from Up North

A black Hall of Fame starting pitcher from Canada who won 20 games every season. That combination qualifies Ferguson Jenkins, one of the best pitchers in Cubs history, as a community of one.

Personable, friendly, and an avid fisherman, Jenkins is among the most approachable of great Cubs players of the past, and he travels so much, there's just no telling where you will run into him.

During the summer of 2004, Jenkins made an appearance on behalf of the Hall of Fame in Fairbanks, Alaska. He threw out a special mid-game, midnight pitch at the Midnight Sun Baseball Game, the only game played with a first pitch at 10:30 PM where field lights have never been turned on. The century-old tradition is possible because the game is played on the longest day of the year each June in the far north.

During the summer of 2005, Jenkins could be found signing auto graphs at the National Sports Card Collectors Convention in the Chicago suburb of Rosemont. Or playing golf at Lake Geneva, Wisconsin. Hall of Fame official Greg Harris said, "Fergie does put in the miles." Jenkins himself said, "I like to travel."

When he was younger, Jenkins, who was born in Chatham, Ontario, in 1942, liked to strike people out, win baseball games, and finish what he started. Jenkins, the 6'5" flamethrower, won 20 games for the Cubs six seasons in a row between 1967 and 1972. His victory totals were: 20, 20, 21, 22, 24, and 20. Jenkins also recorded 20 or more complete games in those seasons with a high of 30 in 1971. These days, it is headline news when a starting pitcher goes the full nine innings, and it is rare for a starter to pitch five complete games in a season. Jenkins had 267 complete games in a career that spanned from 1965 to 1983. He also struck out 3,192 batters.

DID YOU KNOW . . .

That among the Cubs memorabilia housed at the Baseball Hall of Fame in Cooperstown is an undershirt autographed by pitcher Ferguson Jenkins?

In all, Jenkins won 284 games in his career, 167 of them for the Cubs. He also pitched for the Philadelphia Phillies, Texas Rangers, and Boston Red Sox, but in retirement is more closely aligned with the Cubs.

"I played 10 years with them," Jenkins said. "When I came over in a trade in 1966, Leo Durocher had me in the bullpen at the beginning of the season. Then I became a starter. I just proved I could do different things and that a starting role fit me better than the bullpen. Winning 20 games six years in a row kind of told people I could play and I could win."

Jenkins said he believes the fans always understood that owner P. K. Wrigley had their best interests at heart and that he was also a fan who wanted the club to do well.

"They had great fans and even more so in 1968 and 1969 when we started to win," Jenkins said. "I think the people really understood that the organization under Mr. Wrigley had a great ballclub. The people who come out to the ballpark know there is a lot of nostalgia there. They sit on those rooftops. They just love to be present at the ballpark. It's a fun place to be. I think the fans don't even look to the ballclub to win as much as they love to be there.

"The ballpark is over 90 years old. It's in a neighborhood that has changed from different ethnic cultures. All of that endures. It's gone from Jewish to Polish to Italian to Spanish on the North Side. Now it's called Wrigleyville. All of a sudden, someone decided to call it 'Wrigleyville.' To buy homes in that area is really expensive. A lot of these new ballparks change their names because they're bought by big corporations. Wrigley Field has never changed its name, just like Yankee Stadium."

Wrigley Field is very much a part of its neighborhood. It is not easy for that neighborhood to absorb all of the people who arrive for games via the Chicago Transit Authority Red Line elevated train, or to find a place to park all of the cars. It was a tight enough squeeze for the players to park, and when they stepped out of their cars they became part of the neighborhood.

"Back in 1970, driving to the ballpark we turned into the adjacent fire station on Waveland Avenue," Jenkins said. "People would be waiting for

Fastballer Ferguson Jenkins rears back to fire in a 1966 game during which he shut out the Giants. Jenkins produced six straight 20-victory seasons for the Cubs and was voted into the Hall of Fame for his 284 career triumphs.

us to come for day games at 9:30 or 10:00 AM. They'd pat us on the back, shake our hand. That was the fun part of playing at Wrigley Field."

That closeness with the fans has all but evaporated in most cities and circumstances. Big league ballplayers often act big-headedly, and 35 years later there is more of a remove from the fans.

"I just think basically times have changed," Jenkins said. "Now the players park in a parking lot, fenced in. They don't sign autographs, which is somewhat different than the way we did things in the '60s and '70s. The fans don't see the players up front as much as possible."

Jenkins was part of good Cubs teams, was one of the leaders, and he enjoyed being around the always cheerful Ernie Banks and what he calls the usually "flamboyant" Ron Santo.

"He was the captain of our ballclub," Jenkins said. "Not too many ballclubs have captains, but Ronnie was our captain. Ronnie was in a good mood, upbeat, almost more than Ernie [Banks]."

Not only is starting and finishing games almost a lost art, but with pitchers in a five-day rotation rather than the old four-day rotation, it is more challenging for them to win 20 games in a season. Forget pitchers winning 20 games six years in a row as Jenkins did. It's more likely the designated hitter will be abolished.

"I don't think that's going to happen," Jenkins said of streaks of 20-victory seasons and a return to more complete games. "I was getting 35 and 40 starts a season. I think I had 30 [actually, 29] complete games with the Texas Rangers once, too. Yep, it's a lost deal.

"The bullpens are so strong now. All of the strategies are on the bullpens. They have a holder, a setup man, and a closer. You have three guys that are capable of closing ballgames, so they only want a starter to pitch six innings. The pitch count is so prevalent in the game of baseball now. It was unheard of when I played. I might throw 150 or 160 pitches."

For those very reasons, it has been suggested that the era of a 300-game winner in the majors may be over. It is a little-known fact that

By the NUMBERS

1—Until 1932, Cubs uniforms did not display numbers on the backs of jerseys. The first No. 1 was Woody English, who was given the number that season. Other Cubs players to wear No. 1 are Dave Martinez, Augie Ojeda, Kenny Lofton, and Jose Macias.

20-game winners who can accumulate close to that many triumphs are an extreme rarity among black pitchers. Jenkins is one of only 13 black pitchers to ever win 20 games in a major league season even once.

Jenkins is a rarity in several ways.

TRIVIA

Who was the only Cubs player to be named MVP in the All-Star Game?

Answers to the trivia questions are on pages 158–159.

Not only is he one of the greatest Cubs players of all time, he is among the greatest black starting pitchers of all time and the winningest, with his name inscribed on the 1971 Cy Young Award, as well. He is also the only Canadian in baseball's Hall of Fame. An all-around athlete, Jenkins in the 1960s played basketball a few off-seasons for the Harlem Globetrotters. Later, he raised horses on a 160-acre spread in Oklahoma and became commissioner of the Canadian Baseball League.

When he was a youngster, Jenkins played hockey, as most young Canadian lads do. But he also learned how to hunt and fish and has kept up his fishing throughout adulthood. In the summer of 2004, while in Alaska, Jenkins hauled in a 50-pound king salmon—and yes, there were witnesses. When he played with the Cubs, Jenkins often fished with outfielder Billy Williams, another fishing aficionado.

"I definitely made time for it," Jenkins said.

And despite his hectic schedule in so-called retirement, Jenkins still makes time for fishing. He does his best to sneak away to Canada to capture northern pike, muskie, and bass. The big man enjoys catching big fish.

A Surprise MVP and the Rise of the New Cubs

Andre Dawson was determined. When he became a free agent he knew exactly what team he wanted to join—the Chicago Cubs. Although the former Montreal Expos star seemed to have his pick of clubs, he had his reasons.

Dawson had bad knees and he was an aging outfielder who thought the unique combination of Wrigley Field and the Cubs would help him.

"Coming to Chicago, playing the day games, was an effort to extend my playing career," Dawson said. "Chicago came to mind first, too, because Wrigley was a natural playing surface."

It was a trying time in Dawson's personal life. His grandmother had just died.

"I reflected on a lot of things," he said. "I put a lot of things into perspective. I wanted to have fun."

Dawson wanted to play for the Cubs so badly he presented the team with a blank contract and told team officials to fill in the amount they felt was fair to pay him. The Cubs paid Dawson $500,000 for the 1987 season, and it was a bargain. He won the Most Valuable Player award. Dawson hit 49 home runs with 137 runs batted in and played right field for the Cubs for six years. He became a widely popular player with Cubs fans.

"The fans kind of embraced me from day one and gave me the feeling I belonged," Dawson said. "I kind of got in a rhythm seeing the ball better. The fans in Chicago are the best, without a doubt, unless you're having a problem. Fans don't mind your making an error or striking out. They're not spoiled at all. They yearn for postseason play. They were the best fans I ever played for."

Indeed, Cubs fans did and do yearn for postseason play. Any October baseball is as welcome as a winning lottery ticket. In fact, the odds on having winning lottery tickets and Cubs postseason play are probably equivalent.

The summer of 1983, when the Cubs finished 71–91, offered little in the way of a breakthrough hint. The highlight, if it can be called that, was manager Lee Elia's rant against the fans. Those who heard it were amazed. Those who read about it were enraged. It was a gem of a tirade, inspired by fan booing and fans who dumped beer on a couple of players. It likely contributed to Elia being fired in the middle of the season.

The Speech, not to be confused with the Gettysburg Address, went like this: "F*ck those f*ckin' fans who come out here and say they're Cub fans that are supposed to be behind you rippin' every f*ckin' thing you do. I'll tell you one f*ckin' thing, I hope we get f*ckin' hotter than shit, just to stuff it up them 3,000 f*ckin' people that show up every f*ckin' day, because if they're the real Chicago f*ckin' fans, they can kiss my f*ckin' ass right downtown—and *print it!*"

Elia went on. "The motherf*ckers don't even work. That's why they're out at the f*ckin' game. They oughta go out and get a f*ckin' job and find out what it's like to go out and earn a f*ckin' living. Eighty-five percent of the f*ckin' world is working. The other 15 come out here—a f*ckin' playground for the cocksuckers. Rip them motherf*ckers! Rip them f*ckin' cocksuckers like the f*ckin' players!"

Elia went on some more. But that was enough. Elia went off on April 29 and he was bleeped out of town on August 22. In his own way, Elia rivaled the poetry of Tinker to Evers to Chance.

Who would have expected that the Cubs were on the brink of something special? One season later, Chicago finished 96–65 under Jim Frey, obtaining their first postseason appearance in 39 years. This was the season second baseman Ryne Sandberg, a throw-in part of a trade with

By the NUMBERS

42—The last Cubs on-field individual to wear No. 42 before Major League Baseball retired the number throughout the game in order to honor Jackie Robinson was coach Dan Madison, who displayed the numeral from 1995 to 1997.

TRIVIA

Who are the four Cubs players who have won the National League Rookie of the Year award?

Answers to the trivia questions are on pages 158–159.

the Phillies two years before, emerged as a star. He batted .314 with 200 hits, smacked 19 triples and 19 homers, while stealing 32 bases, and won the National League's Most Valuable Player award.

Sandberg's season was highlighted by a stupendous performance on June 23 that is forever remembered in Cubs World as "the Sandberg Game." In a 12–11 victory over the Cardinals, Sandberg hit two home runs and three singles and drove in seven runs. The extraordinary numbers speak for themselves, but Sandberg distinguished himself further by the timing of his big swats. He hit a solo homer to tie the game 9–9 in the ninth and a two-run homer to tie it 11–11 in the tenth inning before the Cubs won in the eleventh.

One of the other remarkable developments of the summer was the Cubs' acquisition of pitcher Rick Sutcliffe on June 13. Sutcliffe went 16–1 for the Cubs the rest of the way and won the Cy Young Award.

The excitement generated by the surprisingly lively Cubs enthralled their fans. The team set a new attendance record by attracting 2,104,219 fans to Wrigley Field. It heralded the beginning of a new era for the team when sellouts at the old ball yard became commonplace. Less than a generation later the Cubs were drawing 3 million fans per season.

Many longstanding institutions were undergoing change in Cubs World. After P. K. Wrigley died, his heirs struggled with inheritance taxes. On June 16, 1981, the chewing gum family let the precious possession out of its hands, selling the Cubs, complete with Wrigley real estate, to the Tribune Company, parent corporation of the *Chicago Tribune*, for $20.5 million.

Earlier that spring, the WGN Superstation ushered in a new era of Cubs television viewing. WGN was seen in homes across the country. Suddenly, baseball fans who had never set foot in Chicago, who only knew it as the place where Mrs. O'Leary's cow kicked over a lantern and started a big fire, became Cubs fans. They began making pilgrimages to see the team they rooted for from afar and to visit the holy temple of Wrigley Field. Before you knew it, there were Cubs fans everywhere in the nation.

Ryne Sandberg was both a spectacular fielder and a surprisingly powerful hitter for the Cubs, setting the all-time record for most home runs by a second baseman (since broken). Shown here belting a home run in 1997 on the day he announced his retirement, Sandberg was enshrined in the Hall of Fame in 2005.

This creative and visionary packaging of cable TV and major league baseball was propelled forward with a major boost when team owners hired Harry Caray as the featured Cubs broadcaster. The loud, funny, enthusiastic, sometimes off-the-wall fan favorite who had long runs with both of the Cubs' biggest rivals, the St. Louis Cardinals and Chicago

Hard-charging Mark Grace collides with Phillies catcher Mike Lieberthal during a 1998 game. Grace was a slick-fielding, timely hitting first baseman for the Cubs between 1988 and 2000.

White Sox, was an inspired choice. Caray, who was in exile for a season broadcasting Oakland A's games, had long been a regional icon. Soon he was a national figure and ultimately became beloved wherever Cubs baseball was viewed. The reach of WGN rivaled the proliferation of McDonald's restaurants. That meant Harry Caray had nearly as wide a viewership as the president making his State of the Union Address—only Caray was on every day for six months. Caray became the face of the franchise and, as he would put it, "Holy Cow!" held sway over Cubs World for the last 16 years of his life.

"Harry was like a pied piper," Dawson said. "Fans wanted to see Harry. Harry was special. And WGN, I think that's why you have so many Cubs fans. You watch 'em day in and day out and you develop something."

Dawson personally experienced how far the tentacles of WGN stretched once when he took a vacation to the Bahamas. He thought he could blend in and be anonymous among the other beachgoers. Nope.

"I found out they were big Cubs fans and big Andre Dawson fans because of WGN," he said. "That was surprising to me. You're on an island and expect to vacation. I thought, 'I'm still in the States, I guess.' I signed lots of autographs."

Dawson was not the only one initially oblivious to the impact that WGN made. Jerome Holtzman, the sportswriter, said nobody in Chicago was really up to date, that new Cubs fans were being created all over far-flung harbors and villages of the United States.

"We were not aware of it," Holtzman said. "Only the Cubs executives. People in Chicago were unaware of it."

The Cubs revolution truly exploded in 1984. WGN had 8 million viewers, and when the team was a champion, to boot, fans became more rabid. Acknowledging that the Curse of the Billy Goat might be genuine, early in April of the 1982 season an attempt to reverse it was made. Sam Sianis, nephew of William who had cursed the club in 1945 for not allowing him to bring his goat into Wrigley, tried to undo the damage. Sam Sianis brought a new goat into the park. It took two years, however, before even the inkling of a curse reverse was in the offing.

In 1984 Chicago was poised for a World Series. The Cubs and the fans were hungry for a return to the big stage for the first time since 1945, and

IF ONLY . . . Leon Durham had worn a new glove onto the field during the 1984 playoffs against San Diego. If Durham had made the putout at first, the Cubs could have changed history, advancing to the World Series.

dare anyone say it, the first World Series title since 1908. Of course, none of that came to pass. The doings made the superstitious even more paranoid that a curse lived on.

The Cubs won their division and moved on to a series against the San Diego Padres, the winner to go to the Series. The Cubs won the first game 13–0. Oh, the fans were delirious. The Cubs won the second game 4–2. Not only were World Series tickets printed, fans started to believe an appearance in the Series was a birthright. To Cubs fans' disbelief and despair, the team promptly lost to the Padres 7–1, 7–5, and 6–3, and were eliminated from the best-of-five playoff.

"We had them by the throat and let them go," lamented Cubs general manager Dallas Green, the architect of the success who assembled the club through a multitude of trades.

The Cubs were leading 3–2 into the seventh inning of the fifth game when a ground ball rolled through the legs of first baseman Leon "Bull" Durham, respected power hitter with (it was speculated) a glove encased in cement. The sentiment was not all wrong. Durham revealed that someone in the dugout spilled Gatorade on his glove, stiffening it. He did not mention the flavor. Boston Red Sox backers blamed the 1986 World Series defeat on Bill Buckner's botching of a grounder at first. The Cubs matched their symbiotic American League counterpart with Durham.

Green, who managed the Philadelphia Phillies to their only World Series championship in 1980, was known to be a bit direct, even harsh, in his comments to players and journalists. It was hard to top his 1986 dismissal of pitching coach Billy Connors, however. The story goes like this: the Cubs were back in the dungeon with a 70–90 record that season, and the team's earned-run average was lousy. Connors was in the hospital recovering from surgery. Did Green drop by to deliver a card? Flowers? Heck no. He left his car running, ran up to Connors' room, fired him, and then returned to the vehicle with the percolating motor. Perhaps he just didn't have change for a meter.

Bargain pickup Andre Dawson won the Most Valuable Player award in 1987 after coming off the free-agent market from Montreal and signing cheaply with the Cubs. Dawson wanted to play day games and patrol the grass outfield at Wrigley Field to help preserve his knees.

TOP TEN

Cubs Career Home-Run Leaders

Name	Home Runs
1. Sammy Sosa	545
2. Ernie Banks	512
3. Billy Williams	392
4. Ron Santo	337
5. Ryne Sandberg	282
6. Gabby Hartnett	231
7. Bill Nicholson	205
8. Hank Sauer	198
9. Hack Wilson	190
10. Andre Dawson	174

After their brief flirtation with the limelight, the Cubs settled back into the nether regions of the National League. That is until 1989, when the club put together another run from nowhere, finishing 93–69 and winning their division under manager Don Zimmer.

First baseman Mark Grace, who would be a very consistent .300 hitter for the Cubs for years; Sandberg; and a young pitcher named Greg Maddux, who won 19 games, led the team during the happy season. Major contributions also came from relief pitcher Mitch Williams. Williams was a thrill-a-minute guy. He filled the bases before pulling off a Houdini-like escape without allowing any runs. He said unpredictable things such as, "I pitch like my hair is on fire." There is no way to chart how edgy he made his manager and coaches, or the fans.

Williams' nickname was "Wild Thing" and he more than lived up to it as the real-life counterpart to the movie part played by Charlie Sheen in *Major League*. In the film, Sheen enters games to the strains of the song "Wild Thing."

Naturally, the Cubs preserved their reputation of piling heartburn on top of heartache when they lost the National League Championship Series to the San Francisco Giants four games to one.

Dawson was part of that run, collecting his 2,000[th] hit during the 1989 season. Although his association with the Florida Marlins, for whom he is now special assistant to the president, gave him a World Series ring in 2003, he is still most closely associated with the Cubs.

"Probably I made my awareness with lots of fans through the Cubs," Dawson said. "I still have a lot of ties in Chicago. Chicago was like a second home. I feel that the Cubs are not that far away from a World Series now. It would be surreal. I think I'd make sure to have reservations."

Actually, it's a safe bet that the Cubs would find a way to make room for one of their MVPs at Wrigley if they reach the World Series.

Harry Caray,
the Talking Machine

There has never been anyone like him. Harry Caray was Mr. Baseball wherever he broadcast. His style was part radio man, part baseball fan, part home team man. He told his observation of the truth with such bluntness that often it hurt the manager or players. He was a critic who offered from-the-heart critiques and a homer who root, root, rooted for the home team.

He mispronounced players' names, yet everyone knew what he meant. When he appeared at some event like the annual Cubs Convention, he was greeted like a white-haired rock star beloved by all breeds of fan.

When a Cubs victory was sealed, Caray proclaimed, "Cubs win! Cubs win!" When the ball was shooting off a Cubs bat and headed toward the outfield wall for a home run, he said, "It might be…it could be…it is! A home run!" He also regularly said, "You can't beat fun at the old ballpark." Caray was certainly someone who contributed to that fun.

And whenever he was astonished by something on the field and wished to convey the emotion to the fans, Caray shouted, "Holy Cow!" The name of his autobiography, written with *Chicago Tribune* columnist Bob Verdi, is *Holy Cow!*, and in 1999 the phrase was patented.

Over the years, he hung out with Elvis Presley and partied so late and so long that he was anointed the Mayor of Rush Street for his clubbing. Harry Caray was one of a kind who personally elevated "Take Me Out to the Ballgame" into baseball's true anthem.

His outsized personality helped grow the Cubs' fan base in the 1980s and 1990s, and while he was living large and loving it, the millions of fans who listened to him in Chicago and around the country understood it was a nonstop, season-long bash and rolled along with him.

Despite working 53 years in the broadcast booth for the St. Louis Cardinals (25 years), the Chicago White Sox (11), the Oakland A's (1), and ultimately the Cubs for the last 16 years of his life, Caray never lost his youthful exuberance for the game, and the fans sensed it. He often said he had done well in this life for an orphan from St. Louis. Fans felt he was one of them and yet also the narrator of a great stage play linked to the game and Wrigley Field. Some people even said he was bigger than the games he broadcast, that his showmanship, especially during the seventh-inning stretch leading fans in singing "Take Me Out to the Ballgame," was as big a draw as the team.

Caray always disagreed with that analysis, and in the last major interview of his life, with *Chicago Tribune* sportswriter Paul Sullivan, he explained that view.

"A lot of people say that and some of them are people of stature," Caray said. "And that makes me feel good. But I don't buy that. I don't think the announcer can do that. The fan comes to see the player. What the announcer can do is make it so interesting that the fan has the desire to come see the players."

"Let me hear ya! A one...a two...a three...." The image of Caray leaning out of the press box at Wrigley to lead the fans in song for the seventh-inning stretch is a vivid one imprinted on fans' minds forever. The simple tune so closely identified with baseball for decades (if not quite so consistently popular) became his signature.

It was Bill Veeck, the flamboyant, spectator-friendly owner of the White Sox, who dreamed up the idea that Caray should sing "Take Me Out to the Ballgame" over the Comiskey Park loudspeaker. When he broached the plan to Caray, however, the broadcaster rebuffed him. Finally, unbeknownst to Caray, Veeck had Caray's microphone hooked into the old Comiskey sound system, and Caray discovered his voice booming throughout the park. The move was an instant smash with the fans, and Veeck and Caray kept it up. When Caray moved to the Cubs in 1982, his sing-along was a staple.

By the NUMBERS 6—That's how many broadcasters who spent some time with the Cubs are in the baseball Hall of Fame. They are: Bob Elson, Russ Hodges, Jack Brickhouse, Harry Caray, Milo Hamilton, and Jimmy Dudley.

"Take Me Out to the Ballgame" is a slice of Americana written in 1908 by a songwriter named Jack Norworth. One day, Norworth was riding the subway in New York and saw an ad for Giants games at the Polo Grounds. He wrote the song in half an hour. The words were set to music by Norworth partner Albert Von Tilzer, and they were optimistic it would be a popular hit in conjunction with the Detroit Tigers–Cubs World Series of that autumn. Yet it did not sell as well as they hoped. Neither did it rival Norworth's biggest hit "Shine on Harvest Moon," cowritten with his wife, Norah Bayes.

Given that there is only a minute or so between innings, only the chorus of "Take Me Out to the Ballgame" is routinely sung during the seventh-inning stretch. It has been said that 99 percent of Americans know of "Take Me Out to the Ballgame," but it is just as likely that 99 percent of the people who think they know the lyrics are unaware of the full, long version.

The entire song goes like this:

Katie Casey was baseball mad, had the fever and had it bad;
Just to root for the home town crew, ev'ry sou Katie blew.
On a Saturday, her young beau called to see if she'd like to go,
To see a show but Miss Kate said, "No, I'll tell you what you can do":

Take me out to the ballgame, take me out with the crowd,
Buy me some peanuts and Cracker Jack, I don't care if I never get back.
Let me root, root, root for the home team, if they don't win, it's a shame.
For it's one, two, three strikes you're out at the old ballgame.

Katie Casey saw all the games, knew the players by their first names;
Told the umpire he was wrong, all along, good and strong.
When the score was just two to two, Katie Casey knew what to do,
Just to cheer up the boys she knew, she made the gang sing this song:

Take me out to the ballgame, take me out with the crowd,
Buy me some peanuts and Cracker Jack, I don't care if I never get back,

TOP TEN

Cubs Single-Season Stolen Bases (since 1900)

	Name	Year	Stolen Bases
1.	Frank Chance	1903	67
2.	Bill Maloney	1905	59
3.	Frank Chance	1906	57
4.	Ryne Sandberg	1985	54†
	Eric Young	2000	54†
6.	Johnny Evers	1906	49
7.	Davey Lopes	1985	47
8.	Johnny Evers	1907	46
9.	Bob Dernier	1984	45
10.	Ivan DeJesus	1980	44

Let me root, root, root for the home team, if they don't win it's a shame.

For it's one, two, three strikes you're out at the old ballgame.

Ironically, Norworth was not particularly a rabid baseball fan and did not actually attend a major league game until 1942, 34 years after he wrote "Take Me Out to the Ballgame."

Over time, the song was tinkered with, and Katie Casey's name was changed to Nelly Kelly in 1927. It was never publicly established just who Katie Casey or Nelly Kelly were. They may have been acquaintances of Norworth—old girlfriends—or they may have been fictional characters.

Caray, whose son Skip became a baseball announcer, as did his grandson Chip, joined the Cubs after longtime legendary broadcaster Jack Brickhouse retired. Brickhouse, whose trademark home run call was "Hey-Hey!" called Cubs games from 1941 to 1981 and he was a soothing companion compared to Caray's rambunctious style. Yet he was a great admirer of his polar opposite.

In the book, *I Remember Harry Caray* by Rich Wolfe and George Castle, Brickhouse, who died in 1998 at the age of 82, said of Caray, "He was a guaranteed audience builder. He was his own man. Harry never copied anybody."

Wolfe himself wrote that the seventh inning was "Caray-oke" time. Perfect.

It was appropriate that Harry Caray, who ate and drank into the wee hours all over Chicago as he told stories and schmoozed with celebrities and baseball fans from all walks of life, would open his own restaurant. The restaurant in downtown Chicago opened on November 1, 1987, and

Harry Caray, the legendary broadcaster, leading the fans at Wrigley Field in a rendition of "Take Me Out to the Ballgame" during the seventh-inning stretch. The daily ritual was wildly popular and continues today with celebrity guest singers following in the late Caray's footsteps.

as proof that the legend behind it and the food from its kitchen are both going strong, it was still doing a booming business seven years after Caray's death.

Not surprisingly, the restaurant has a baseball decor. There are innumerable photographs of baseball players and actors, many of them autographed, many of the subjects posed with Caray. There are pictures of Caray with President Ronald Reagan, a one-time sportscaster himself, Mike Ditka, Tommy Lasorda, and others. There are framed newspaper clippings and Caray mementos, plaques, and awards in glass cases. The place is a shrine to Caray with first-rate food and it describes itself as an Italian steakhouse.

Outside Wrigley Field, at the corner of Addison and Sheffield, stands a Harry Caray statue. Caray towers above fans peeking out from the grandstand walls of Wrigley, waving a mike in his hand. At Harry Caray's Restaurant, replicas of the sculpture sell for $99.95.

When he was younger, Caray purposely fooled around with players' names in his broadcasts. When he was older (and there was some dispute over his age, though it was likely 78 or older), Caray's malapropisms or mangling of names garnered attention. He called Andre Dawson "Andre Rodgers," called Orioles star Eddie Murray "Eddie Murphy," and referred to famed Cubs slugger Sammy Sosa as "Sammy Sofa."

"Harry Caray was remarkable," said Cubs ex-star second baseman Glenn Beckert. "He had some great stories in his life. He was a remarkable guy. I don't think a lot of players appreciated him when they were playing because he could be rough on players. But he did a great job."

Caray, who in 1987 had a stroke and missed time in the broadcast booth, collapsed at a nightclub in California from a heart problem on Valentine's Day of 1998 while dining with his wife Dutchie, and he died a few days later on February 18. At his funeral, "Take Me Out to the Ballgame" was played on bagpipes.

Bill Murray, the actor and former *Saturday Night Live* star who is a longtime Cubs fan, helped fill in for Caray when he had his stroke and was somber, yet appropriately lightly sardonic when he died.

"Well, I'm glad he went out in a bar, anyway," Murray told the *Chicago Tribune.* "It was very sad news. You always dread the day when somebody like [Caray] goes."

That when broadcaster Harry Caray joined the White Sox in 1971, his contract was set up with an escalator clause based on team attendance? He earned bonuses based on how many fans came to the games.

After his death, there was an outpouring of praise for Caray, who like Brickhouse, is in the broadcast wing of the baseball Hall of Fame. Sosa said everyone in the Dominican Republic loved him. Present-day Cubs pitcher Kerry Wood said he grew up in Texas watching Caray because he never knew what he would say.

Tributes in the *Chicago Tribune* after Caray's death were legion. TV analyst Steve Stone, who worked with Caray for 16 years, said, "He was truly unique in a profession where everyone sounds the same. You could close your eyes and always tell it was Harry."

Ernie Banks said when he hit his first home run, Caray was broadcasting for the Cardinals and the next day told him he was going to be a great hitter. He said Caray's voice was a powerful sales tool for baseball and that even though fans and experts refer to Banks as a terrific baseball ambassador, "He was greater."

It might be said that Caray is still selling the game from the grave. Caray had become nationally identified with the Cubs through WGN cable broadcasts, and many said that he brought fans out to the park with his "Take Me Out to the Ballgame" renditions. In the years since his death, the Cubs have carried on the tradition. Being asked to lead the seventh-inning stretch singing at Wrigley Field is regarded as a great compliment.

Among those who have sung are: Bill Murray, singer Billy Corgan of Smashing Pumpkins, Ozzy Osbourne, Dick Vitale, Vin Scully, Nancy Kerrigan, Jackie Mason, Jack Black, Russell Crowe, Dwyane Wade, Kid Rock, Cuba Gooding Jr., Dallas Green, Mike Ditka, Bill Buckner, Eddie Vedder of Pearl Jam, and Bernie Mac. The first invited to sing in the new season after Caray passed away was his wife Dutchie.

Many former Cubs have also played the part. They slip on a Cubs jersey once again, take the microphone, and sing, sometimes off-key, sometimes surprisingly well.

"It's a great kick," said Beckert, who sang during the summer of 2005. "People are interested."

Hall of Fame outfielder Billy Williams came from a singing family and has led "Take Me Out to the Ballgame" singalongs several times.

"I was one of the first to do it from the baseball field when I was a coach for the Cubs," Williams said. "I did it from the on-deck circle. You don't have to be the greatest singer in the world. Just get up there and perform. All they want is for the person to sing 'Root, root, root for the Cubs.' The guys have a great time up there."

Ditka has proven he is unlikely to make the transition to recording artist in his singalongs, though he performs with gusto. Race car driver Jeff Gordon has had better days going around in circles than he did singing at Wrigley. Osbourne's rendition became notorious when he forgot the words.

Usually, the fans sing with feeling, shouting out the words with laughter and emotion. Corgan, a serious Cubs fan, drew the unenviable assignment of leading "Take Me Out to the Ballgame" for the seventh game of the National League Championship Series against the Florida Marlins. The day before the Cubs had blown their lead in the series and a sense of doom pervaded the North Side.

"That was like singing for a funeral," Corgan said in *Cubs Nation* by Gene Wojciechowski. "It really was like a wake."

Ferguson Jenkins, the great Cubs pitcher, views the opportunity much like Williams does. Jenkins, who sang in Baptist choirs as a youth, has led the singing about half a dozen times.

TRIVIA

Which three Cubs managers have led the National League in the All-Star Game?

Answers to the trivia questions are on pages 158–159.

"'Take Me Out to the Ballgame' is not hard to do," Jenkins said. "It's a lot of fun to get back and see the fans."

Besides former Cubs players, who are welcomed warmly, another regular "Take Me Out to the Ballgame" singer is Tom Dreesen, a comedian who was a long-time Frank Sinatra opening act.

"When you sing like me, you know what a singer is," Dreesen said after leading the crowd during the summer of 2005 for his fifth time. "It's the most exhilarating thing. What a wonderful tribute to Harry and what a great idea. Harry was such a bad singer, he set the precedent. The last time I did it, I followed Ditka, so I was like Pavarotti."

At the time, Dreesen had a friend singing professionally across town in Chicago to a sold-out house of 300 people. He told him, "I've got 38,000."

Harry Caray always had fun, and people always had fun around him. In the bar of Harry Caray's Restaurant, periodically a videotape comes on a screen showing Caray leading the crowd at Wrigley in "Take Me Out to the Ballgame." It is a taste of Caray for those who missed the real thing in person and for those who miss him now.

In between sips of their drinks, patrons just might be tempted to shout, "Holy Cow!"

Let There Be Light

The Cubs saw the light decades after most major league clubs did. Throughout the 1930s, 1940s, 1950s, 1960s, and 1970s, the Cubs and Wrigley Field played the old-fashioned way—in the middle of the day.

However, Major League Baseball had long recognized that, by playing most of its games at night, it would occupy a post-work, leisure-time segment of fans' days, and garner a bigger audience with after-dinner watchers. The idea that in the face of progress the Cubs would stick to the tried-and-true plan that traced to the early days of the game, was seen as quaint. Day baseball was a local quirk. Many players and sportswriters loved it because day games turned their work days into 9-to-5 jobs instead of late-nighters with weird meal times.

Many also theorized that playing all day games, through the heat of the summer, when other teams had an advantage of playing games in the cool of the evening, cost the Cubs the ultimate playoff and World Series success it coveted.

Jay Johnstone, the 1980s outfielder, said playing the field was tough in bright sunshine.

"There can be so much glare you can't even see the ball," he said.

And first baseman Bill Buckner, who played for the Cubs between 1977 and 1984, said, "The Cubs will never win the pennant playing day games."

The first night game in major league history was played at Cincinnati's Crosley Field on May 24, 1935. It was such a big deal that President Franklin Delano Roosevelt was rigged up somehow to throw the switch from Washington.

Former owner P. K. Wrigley had quietly made plans to erect lights at Wrigley Field for the 1942 season. He amassed the metal and the wiring and had it stored in the park. However, when the Japanese bombed Pearl Harbor on December 7, 1941, and the United States entered the Second World War, he donated the materials to the War Department. Four decades passed before the Cubs again seriously entertained the idea of adding night games to their schedule.

In late December of 1981 the Cubs ordered a feasibility study to determine the best way to introduce lights at Wrigley. General Manager Dallas Green became the front man arguing for the importance of lights to the team.

Wrigleyville residents fought back, claiming that night baseball would be bad for the residential neighborhood surrounding the park. Politicians jumped in. The Illinois General Assembly sponsored legislation, and Governor James Thompson signed a law that called for noise pollution standards that only applied to Wrigley. The Chicago City Council leapt in with its own restrictive ordinance on night athletic contests in arenas that by wild coincidence only matched the description of Wrigley Field.

Major League Baseball was tiring of the Cubs' status as the only team without lights, and in 1984 Commissioner Peter Ueberroth threatened to move playoff and World Series games from Wrigley if the team did not install them. Baseball wanted the prime-time audience, and other owners wanted the prime revenue. The Tribune Company filed suit to overturn the restrictions on Wrigley.

Over time a compromise was worked out, permitting the Cubs to schedule 18 regular-season games and all playoff games at night. Years later, it remains a comparative rarity for the Cubs to play night baseball at Wrigley.

The first Cubs night game at Wrigley Field was scheduled for August 8, 1988, and just about anyone who was anyone except Thomas Edison was invited. The hullabaloo surrounding the event seemingly matched a millennium party. Such a big deal was made of the occasion it seemed

IF ONLY . . . The Cubs had been able to contain San Francisco Giants first baseman Will Clark, who batted .650 during the National League Championship Series in 1989, they likely would have advanced to their first World Series in 44 years.

Wrigley Field was the last ballpark in the major leagues to install lighting, and even today the Cubs do not play many night games. Fittingly, the landmark ballpark is home to the largest number of day games played each season.

as if the Cubs were moving on the evolutionary scale directly from fire to lasers.

Once the six banks of lights were installed at a cost of $5 million (compared to Cincinnati's initial outlay of $62,000), the Cubs started slowly, playing eight night games in 1988.

The first scheduled game was regarded as so momentous the Cubs issued 550 media credentials. The opponents were the Philadelphia Phillies, but future Hall of Fame third baseman Mike Schmidt did not seem to get into the spirit of the night.

Surveying the pregame scene, Schmidt said, "You'd have thought an extraterrestrial being was going to land on the field. The damned baseball game didn't have a lot of meaning. It was nothing but an excuse to party. If you lived outside Chicago, it didn't mean much."

Schmidt wasn't far off the mark in many ways, though what's wrong with looking for an excuse to party? And, yes, the event was far more important to Chicagoans than Philadelphians. They had been living with admittedly a national treasure, but also basically an as-is Wrigley Field for three-quarters of a century. It certainly was an occasion. For sale at the game were $24.95 silver commemorative medallions. I-want-to-be-there interest was so intense, some fans paid $1,000 for scalped tickets.

TRIVIA

Of the 100 players who spent time at third base for the Cubs since Ron Santo left the team in 1973, whose tenure produced league-leading hitting accomplishments?

Answers to the trivia questions are on pages 158–159.

Schmidt was correct that the game did not have a lot of meaning in the standings. Even worse, it was rained out after both Ernie Banks and Billy Williams threw out "first" pitches and less than four innings were completed. The lightning was brighter than the artificial illumination. Umpires waited until 10:25 PM to call it, so it was apparent they tried. The rain came down long and hard, and Cubs catcher Jody Davis celebrated the special occasion with a popular baseball maneuver periodically invoked in similar circumstances. Davis raced out of the dugout and did bellyflops on the tarp.

The game was essentially replaced with a party. Indeed, to demonstrate that he was the life of the party, a fan wore a homemade light stand on his head—and did a handstand. The next night, when the Cubs bested the New York Mets 6–4, festivities were more subdued. The focus was on the baseball.

Any discussion of modifying Wrigley in any way, or talk flaring up about playing any additional night games, gets the Wrigleyville residents' and politicians' juices going again.

Still, somehow, despite putting in lights, the traditions of the ballpark were preserved, and Wrigley has remained the Friendly Confines.

And the Fans Go Wild

Scott McPherson has season tickets at Wrigley Field under the overhang on the first base side in section 228 and has had them all but one season since 1998. Now in his mid-forties, he grew up in Chicago as a Cubs fan, but is more broad-minded than many, also making room in his heart for the Chicago White Sox when the rooting interests do not collide.

"I'll root for the White Sox over everybody but the Cubs," McPherson said as he sat in his seat during a June 2005 game against the visiting Boston Red Sox. "I'd love to see a crosstown World Series. I'm not a White Sox hater. I'm a Chicago fan." A South Sider would say that a perfect fall afternoon would be "Bears win, White Sox win, Cubs lose."

Speaking of heart, however, McPherson is like many hardcore Cubs supporters. He associates the team with heartbreak.

"The first heartache I really remember is 1969," McPherson said. "I was pretty young. But I was definitely following Ernie Banks and Ron Santo. Then there was the collapse part."

Cubs Don't Win! Cubs Don't Win!

McPherson attended college in Minnesota and was living there watching on TV in 1984 when the Cubs built their two-games-to-none playoff lead over the Padres.

"When they had the 2–0 lead on San Diego," he said, "you started thinking, 'Okay, they're really going to do it.' And they lost three games in a row and there you go."

Cubs Don't Win! Cubs Don't Win!

"In 1989, you had this feeling they were going to win every game," said McPherson, who is a Chicago public affairs lobbyist. "They pretty much won the division going away."

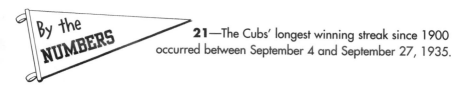

21—The Cubs' longest winning streak since 1900 occurred between September 4 and September 27, 1935.

That season McPherson took a fan tour with complete strangers, all Cubs supporters, to Montreal. There were about 50 of them on hand when the Cubs clinched their playoff spot.

"It was just crazy Cubs fans," McPherson said.

Then the Cubs lost the divisional series to the Giants.

Cubs Don't Win! Cubs Don't Win!

"That was a heartbreak," McPherson said.

On and on Cubs lore goes, always with the punchline being the team losing its last game of the season. In 2003, when the Cubs were five outs from defeating the Florida Marlins and going to the World Series, McPherson jumped the gun. He called his sister in Louisville.

"I said, 'Get your plane ticket,'" he said. " 'We're going to the World Series.' Within 20 minutes it unraveled. It was *sooo* close. It was within your grasp. It really made you think there was some unseen hand.

"I've always been an optimist myself. Usually what happens is that hope springs eternal. Sometimes they were out of it right away because they had a crummy team. Then they'd go and have a spurt and you'd go, 'Maybe they can do it.' It's like a yo-yo."

The Cubs play with their fans' emotions, teasing them with important victories, falling back into the pack with seemingly good teams, being decimated by injuries when experts proclaim they have the best pitching staff in baseball. Yet the fans come in droves, 3 million a season, and they win the admiration of the players they themselves admire.

Shortstop Nomar Garciaparra, the All-Star shortstop acquired from the Boston Red Sox in 2004, said there's nothing like playing in crammed-to-the-gills parks like Fenway and Wrigley.

"I always say what makes them is when the fans are there," Garciaparra said. "They don't become Wrigley or they don't become Fenway until the fans are there. It's nice and great when they're empty, but they are not truly the ballparks until they're filled. And they're filled all of the time. So that's a tribute to the city, to the people who are here a lot. They don't take what they have for granted. They appreciate what they have. They're supportive every day, and we as players appreciate that even more."

In recent years, with the Cubs packing the ballpark for every home game, some fans have taken to traveling in order to see their team. And when they arrive in a foreign city, they discover fresh bands of Cubs fans who grew up watching WGN and being absorbed into Cubs World from afar.

"There are places where it feels like a home game," Garciaparra said. "You go and, wow, it's like we have the home-field advantage. Once again, how do you thank the fans?"

Jerry Hairston Jr., the reserve infielder whose dad played major league ball, grew up in Chicago and understood the Cubs' place in the firmament.

"I knew the Cubs were the biggest thing in town besides Michael Jordan," Hairston said. "We're Chicago's team. People come to the games and have a great time. They fill the park. No question when we go on the road fans are there for us. Sometimes we get a warmer reception than at home."

Manager Dusty Baker, who has been around baseball for four decades, said it amazes him how many Cubs fans there are in other major league cities.

"Twenty-five to 50 percent of the people in the stadium are Cubs fans," he said.

The Cubs fans who come to Wrigley are remarkably consistent, in recent years buying up an entire season's worth of tickets before the first pitch is thrown in April.

The buzz around the field starts hours before game time. The gates open at 5:00 PM for a 7:00 PM start, and just about the first people in line at one gate are two fathers with their sons.

"We want to get autographs," said Cody Wrzesirski, 12, of Midlothian, Illinois, just south of Chicago. Cody's father Roger is a White Sox fan and is not certain how his son adopted the "wrong" team.

"He learned it on his own," Dad said.

The younger Wrzesirski carried a cardboard sign with a message for his favorite player, Cubs first baseman Derrek Lee, who midway through the 2005 season was smacking the ball

TRIVIA

Where does Dusty Baker rank among the winningest active managers?

Answers to the trivia questions are on pages 158–159.

TOP TEN

Cubs Leaders in Career Walks

	Name	Walks
1.	Stan Hack	1,092
2.	Ron Santo	1,071
3.	Cap Anson	952
4.	Mark Grace	946
5.	Billy Williams	911
6.	Sammy Sosa	798
7.	Phil Cavarretta	794
8.	Ernie Banks	763
9.	Ryne Sandberg	761
10.	Bill Nicholson	696

safely at an alarming rate. The sign read, "Go D. Lee—Win the Triple Crown."

His friend Tyler Gulli wore a Mark Prior jersey to advertise his allegiance to the right-handed pitcher.

"I like Prior very much," Gulli said.

The scene around the park was loose, friendly, warm in the summer sun. People wandered in and out of nearby souvenir shops, buying $6 color pictures or long-sleeved Cubs T-shirts priced at $26.

Chicagoan John Baker operated his own business as he strolled outside the park, selling little stuffed animals for the bargain price of $8. They were soft, furry, gray goats wearing blue-and-white-striped blankets emblazoned with the message, "Help Break the Curse."

Baker carried a sign reading, "In with the goat, out with the curse." Supposedly, by investing in the little goat, fans would help eradicate the Billy Goat Curse. There are no other goat salesmen on the street, it appears, and Baker proclaims he is the only one.

"That is a good deal," Baker said.

Baker wore a "Curse Breaker, Help Break the Curse" T-shirt, and a blue Cubs pith helmet with a red C on the front. Of the 2005 Cubs team going nowhere at the time (and ultimately into fourth place), Baker said, "This is not a matter of a curse. This is just a bad baseball team. They're cursed by bad play."

That may be why the Billy Goat Curse was not on anyone's mind. The Cubs seemed to be doing themselves in without outside assistance from a 60-year-old curse. Most of the stuffed animals seemed to remain in their plastic packaging. How are they selling? Baker was asked.

"Frankly, the market sucks," he said.

When the gates opened, a voice came over the public address system.

"Welcome to beautiful Wrigley Field, home of the Chicago Cubs," the voice told early-bird patrons. "We hope you enjoy your visit to the Friendly Confines."

Heartaches aside, more often than not McPherson does enjoy his visits or he wouldn't keep coming back. Still, he has observed with interest the changing nature of Cubs fans, from the more serious baseball fan to an influx of fresh faces who come to Wrigley because it seems trendy.

"I come to watch the game," McPherson said. "I keep score. I know people who show up about the third inning, hang around for a few innings, socialize, and leave. When the Cubs weren't as good, real fans came to the games and there was more room to move around. Now it's a circus. There are still 35,000-plus here on a weekday afternoon. That's a lot. Most of us are working, so it's got to be people from out of town or vacationing.

"It's an effort now to get here and do this. You really have to plan it out. It's been kind of cutthroat. The park wasn't built to handle this load. They need to cut down on the beer drinking so you don't have to spend so much time in the bathroom lines. It's a lot of Johnny-Come-Lately Cubs fans now that they're winning [in 2003 and 2004]. They've probably squeezed out a lot of fans who can't afford it."

Win or lose, McPherson finds experiences at the ballpark to cherish. On the opening day game in the spring after Harry Caray died in 1998, the atmosphere was strange.

"They had this eerie Harry Caray face balloon bobbing around outside the park," McPherson said.

Dutchie Caray was scheduled to lead "Take Me Out to the Ballgame" and McPherson said it was "very emotional."

With two outs in the top of the seventh inning, a chant began. "Harry! Har-ry! Har-ry!"

"I had tears in my eyes," McPherson said.

A Love Tap from the Heart

He ran to right-field with a spring in his step, made a little leap when he belted a home run, and he tapped his heart and waved his love to the fans. Up until the waning days of his long stay in Chicago, Sammy Sosa had one of the great love affairs between a player and a city.

And although it may be sacrilege to some, it can be argued that while Ernie Banks is Mr. Cub, that Sosa is the greatest hitting Cub of them all.

George W. Bush has joked that the greatest mistake he ever made in public life came not while he was governor of Texas or president of the United States, but when he was running the Texas Rangers and traded Sosa to the White Sox before he was moved to the Cubs.

Like many Latin players who made their mark on major league baseball, Sosa came from poverty. He was born November 12, 1968, and grew up in San Pedro de Macoris, Dominican Republic, a community of 125,000 people, where he was a shoeshine boy. The scouts found him, and at 16 Sosa signed with Texas for a $3,500 bonus.

Later, Sosa became a hero in the Dominican Republic for his exploits on the diamond and off it. In 1998, when the island was devastated by a hurricane, Sosa helped mightily with relief work. That was the season when Sosa and St. Louis Cardinals slugger Mark McGwire rejuvenated baseball after a bitter player's strike with their pursuit of Roger Maris' single-season home-run record of 61. Sosa was invited to the White House to meet President Bill Clinton, but called off his visit because he was busy helping the people in his home country. For his work on hurricane relief, Sosa was presented baseball's Roberto Clemente Man of the Year award. On a visit to his home in October of that year, tens of thousands of people turned out to hear Sosa speak. Some were barefoot in the

DID YOU KNOW . . . That Cubs slugger Sammy Sosa won National League Player of the Month five times with the team and won league Player of the Week 11 times?

mud, but they stood patiently in the rain to hear him. Sosa cried as he talked about growing up poor.

"I'm a person touched by God," he said.

For much of his baseball career, after some shaky beginnings, Sosa seemed to be touched by God on the field, too. After a minor league apprenticeship, Sosa had a couple of middling seasons with the White Sox. He blossomed into a regular, then a star, with the Cubs. The first signs of All-Star capability showed through in 1993, when Sosa slugged 33 home runs and drove in 93 runs.

By then, Sosa's outgoing nature, his interaction with the crowds in right field, and his expressive gestures at the plate made him a fan favorite.

"The fans in Chicago love him," said Cubs assistant general manager Ed Lynch in 1995. And that was before Sosa's big years. "He's got a lot of charisma. I think it's just a matter of time before everyone else realizes how good he is."

That time arrived quickly. By the time Sosa smashed 40 homers in 1996, followed by his unprecedented streak of 66 home runs in 1998, 63 in 1999, 50 in 2000, 64 in 2001, and 49 in 2002, he had gone from a $10 million annual salary to about $18 million and was among the biggest names in the sport.

The whole world seemed to love Sammy—and his first name sufficed when referring to him. In fact, during the dual chase of Maris' home-run mark, although McGwire's 70 home runs ended up being the new record, it was Sosa's endearing personality that captivated the nation. He dragged a reluctant McGwire into a brighter spotlight, drawing out the best of McGwire, too. Sosa was determined to have fun, determined to see that McGwire had fun, and determined to make sure the country's baseball fans smiled with him. To a remarkable degree, he succeeded, being perpetually gracious as the pressure mounted, and making innumerable friends for the game. It was a magical summer, and Sosa was in the driver's seat, steering the Cadillac through the confetti of a months-long parade.

Before the season began, it was the hugely muscled McGwire who had the more established persona as home-run slugger, and Sosa bowed to McGwire's prowess.

"Mark McGwire is in a different world," Sosa said. "He's my idol."

Swatting home runs everywhere he traveled—a major league record 20 in June—Sosa excited the average fan, uplifted some of those who had been turned off to the game because of labor strife, and introduced himself to new fans.

"If I keep hitting home runs," he said, "maybe people will like me even more. I feel like I'm just lucky to be in the right place at the right time."

When Sosa hit two home runs on September 13, to tie Maris after McGwire had passed him, and then equaled McGwire at 62 home runs, he told the world he loved McGwire and he had tears in his eyes while reflecting on the accomplishment. Then Sosa hit more home runs.

It was a Woodstock summer of love, a baseball love-in, with Sosa on lead guitar. McGwire ended up with his name beside the single-season record, but it was hard to say that he won the war. Sosa's blasts were just as memorable, he won the RBI title with 158, batted .308, was selected National League MVP, and propelled the Cubs into the playoffs. It was clearly Sammy's time.

Sosa had a clause in his contract calling for a $250,000 payout if he won the MVP—a price tag equal to the original cost of building Wrigley Field. When he was informed of the award, Sosa said all the right things.

"Winning the MVP is not for me," he said. "It's for the people of the city of Chicago."

Club president Andy MacPhail hardly begrudged Sosa the extra cash.

"I'm delighted to pay it," MacPhail said. "Best quarter of a million dollars the company ever spent."

Accolades rolled in and so did rewards. Soon Sosa was collecting an estimated $10 million in endorsements from Pepsi, Montgomery Ward, and Latin American companies. He endorsed Rawlings gloves and Fila

By the NUMBERS .423—The average first baseman Phil Cavarretta compiled to lead the Cubs during the 1945 World Series, their most recent, when the Chicagoans lost four games to three to the Detroit Tigers.

TOP TEN

Cubs Career ERA Leaders
(1,000 Innings Minimum)

Name	ERA
1. Mordecai "Three Finger" Brown	1.80
2. Jack Pfiester	1.85
3. Orval Overall	1.91
4. Ed Reulbach	2.24
5. Larry Corcoran	2.26
6. Hippo Vaughn	2.33
7. Terry Larkin	2.34
8. John Clarkson	2.39
9. Carl Lundgren	2.42
10. Jack Taylor	2.65

sneakers. Sosa lent his name to Slammin' Sammy's Frosted Flakes. He had his own "Wheaties," so to speak. Banks basically said Sosa was the greatest Cub player of all, no small admission, and he liked Sosa.

"He's a wonderful guy," Banks said.

On August 10, 2002, Sosa hit three three-run home runs in a 15–1 victory over the Colorado Rockies, driving in nine runs, despite leaving the game by the sixth inning. The next day Sosa hit a grand slam and drove in five more runs. Sosa is the only player in major league baseball history with three seasons of 60-plus home runs on his résumé. Great stuff, fitting statistical lore to buttress Sosa's reputation as one of the game's great sluggers. He was an actor who provided the fans with top-notch entertainment.

What is remarkable is how quickly it all unraveled, how Sosa the admired became Sosa the resented, how Sosa the beloved became Sosa the unloved, how Sosa the lifelong Cub became an ex-Cub. In a few short years, Sosa went from a guy whom the sports establishment was likely to push for a statue in front of Wrigley to a guy who couldn't get out of town fast enough.

As marvelous a ride as the late 1990s and early 2000s provided, 2003 and 2004 were years Sosa probably wishes could be wiped out with amnesia. Sosa suffered injuries, including a back problem incurred when

During the 1998 season, Sammy Sosa and Mark McGwire energized baseball with their pursuit of Roger Maris' single-season home-run record. Here Sosa watches his 62nd homer disappear over the fence against the Milwaukee Brewers, and then the slugger performed his trademark celebratory hop.

he sneezed too hard. He got into spats with manager Dusty Baker. There was debate about his contract. And Sosa was suspended by Major League Baseball after he broke a bat and its innards were revealed as cork. The incident was hard to swallow or rationalize, even with Sosa's explanation that he had accidentally grabbed a batting practice bat that he used to put on a show for fans.

Although Sosa seemed to recover most of his popularity, at least in Chicago, the relationship between the slugger and the city seemed to go flat. Nationwide, columnists branded Sosa a cheater. Former Cubs teammate Mark Grace, then with the Arizona Diamondbacks, ridiculed Sosa by taping a huge cork to his bat and wielding it before a game with the White Sox. Both Baker and Sosa expressed resentment that Grace would make fun of the matter. Grace said those guys needed to get a sense of humor.

TRIVIA

Who has the Cubs' record for most hits in a single season?

Answers to the trivia questions are on pages 158–159.

But unlike the summer of 1998, there wasn't much laughing around Sosa in 2003 and 2004. If Sosa was previously the king of the clubhouse, the man who swung the big bat and often carried the team on his shoulders, his injury absences reduced his stature. Poor performances when he returned provoked boos from once-adoring fans, and Sosa was deeply hurt. Sosa was criticized about his choice of salsa music on his boom box, was accused of being more interested in individual stats than team success, and sportswriters actually challenged Sosa to take tests to show he was not on steroids.

During the final weeks of the 2004 season, when the Cubs were still alive for the National League wild-card playoff spot, Sosa and Baker squabbled about Sosa's place in the batting order. There was a lot of he said–he said.

A Sosa-Cubs split was hastened after the last day of the regular season. Sosa was not in the lineup, though it was not 100 percent clear if it was his request, or Baker's decision. But he compounded the bad feelings created by his tumultuous season by disappearing right after the game began— and lying about it. Sosa said he stayed around well into the game. However, a parking lot surveillance tape released by the Cubs indicated he left in the first inning. It was bye-bye, Sammy, in more ways than one.

For most of the winter, the Cubs insisted that Sosa would return for the 2005 season. He was under contract—a huge contract—with nearly $18 million due and he had a no-trade clause. But nobody believed Sosa would be there for spring training in Arizona.

In early February the Cubs traded Sosa to the Baltimore Orioles for infielder Jerry Hairston Jr. and two minor leaguers. It was not much of a price for the man who helped save baseball in 1998.

"It is going to be a beautiful year because I am happy and I am hungry," Sosa said. "I'm in a new house. I have to go up there and put it together, show the whole world I have a new challenge and I am taking it."

Sosa spent from 1992 to 2004 with the Cubs. He hit a team record 545 homers, eclipsing Banks, drove in 1,414 runs in a Cubs uniform, and scored 1,245 runs. In 2001 Sosa drove in 160 runs.

Immediately after the trade, Sosa took out a full page ad in the *Chicago Tribune*. It pictured Sosa doffing his cap and a short message: "It's been an honor to play for the best fans in baseball. I was proud to be a Cub. My heartfelt thanks to the Cubs organization, my teammates, and the fans of Chicago for 13 wonderful years. Thank you Chicago—I love you."

It was a gracious gesture, a reminder of the old Sammy, when life was beautiful and it seemed like the marriage of Sammy Sosa and the Cubs would last forever.

There Really Is a Curse

On a display in a glass case near the entrance to Harry Caray's Restaurant are the scorched remains of a baseball. It is a peculiar monument to the desperate inner workings of the Cub fan's mind, muted testimony to the passion, the desire, the disappointment, and fatalism of the job.

It is an artifact from 2003, the scarred remnant of hope, the symbol of Cubs blind belief gone haywire. It represents, in its shredded form, the shattering of a dream in a most painful manner.

The Chicago Cubs were five outs from the World Series in October 2003. It would have been the team's first World Series appearance in 58 years. Instead, a season destined for unimaginable glory ended in ashes, its message of lost love a perpetual ache in the heart of Cubs supporters.

When Dusty Baker was hired as manager of the Cubs on November 19, 2002, he was blissfully ignorant of negative Cubs legends, of billy goats and curses. A baseball man to the core, he saw only a baseball opportunity attached to an ancient franchise with a popular fan base and a marvelous ballpark. Undaunted that the Cubs had not won the National League pennant since 1945, he said, "When I think about it, why not me? Why not us?" Clearly an innocent, Baker didn't realize that his club not only had to win games on the field, it had to beat fate, as well.

In Baker's first season, the Cubs won the National League Central Division with an 88–74 record. That was a pretty good 2003 already. So far, so good. The only real quirky negative was slugger Sammy Sosa being caught with a corked bat on June 3. Sosa's bat broke on a grounder, and the evidence of the illegal substance clogging the wooden club was laid bare for all—including umpires—to see. Many people thought Sosa had cork in

IF ONLY . . . Moises Alou had beaten Steve Bartman to the Florida Marlins' foul ball during the 2003 National League Championship Series. Would Alou have caught it? Would the Cubs have advanced to the World Series? Would the Cubs still have given up eight runs that inning?

his head when he explained it was his batting practice bat accidentally taken from the rack. No other Sosa bats were discovered containing cork. He was thrown out of that 3–2 victory over the Tampa Bay Devil Rays and suspended for 10 games.

The Cubs captured the division and advanced to the playoffs. In the first round they topped the Atlanta Braves, three games to two. It was the team's first postseason series victory since 1908. So far, so good. Next came the Florida Marlins, and after losing the opener, the Cubs swept the next three games, 12–3, 5–4, and 8–3.

Now it looked like a sure thing. Chicago fans were wheeling and dealing for World Series tickets. Not even the club's hapless history held them back. And then the impossible happened. The Marlins won the fifth game. Okay, stuff happens. In the sixth game more bleak adventure happened than fills the 1,500 pages of *War and Peace*.

The Cubs took a 3–0 lead into the eighth inning with ace Mark Prior mowing down hitters. One out. But there was no clock on that second out. Marlins center fielder Juan Pierre doubled and then Luis Castillo lofted a ball down the left-field line, curving toward the seats. Cubs left fielder Moises Alou ran to the wall. Just as Alou was poised to reach over the wall in foul territory to take a stab at the hit, a fan in the first row reached out and sought to catch it.

The fan, a 26-year-old man named Steve Bartman, deflected the ball. Alou flashed disgust, the Wrigley Field crowd booed Bartman incessantly, and security hustled him away. The ball bounced to another fan. Back on the field, Castillo walked, the Marlins erupted, and in a flash Florida had eight runs on the board. The Marlins won and took Game 7 a day later, before sweeping to a World Series title. Cubs fans are still in shock.

Repercussions were swift. Bartman, garbed in glasses, a Cubs hat, a blue sweatshirt, and wearing earphones, was only trying to grab a souvenir

Left fielder Moises Alou seeks to catch a foul ball in the 2003 playoffs against the Florida Marlins, but fan Steve Bartman (Cubs cap, earphones) tries to obtain a souvenir, and the ball falls into the seats. The Cubs subsequently blew their chance to advance to the World Series by losing this game and the next.

foul ball. Alou portentously said afterward, "I hope he doesn't regret it the rest of his life." Baker suggested that perhaps the transgressor was a Marlins fan. Quickly, TV crews ferreted out Bartman's residence and set up cameras on the lawn. Aware of the hostility, the lifelong Cubs fan wisely refused interviews, stayed out of sight, and issued an apology. The kindest thing said about Bartman was that he was stupid.

A day after his fielding miscue, Bartman issued a statement that read in part, "I am so truly sorry from the bottom of this Cub fan's broken heart." He said he had his eyes on the ball and had no idea the ball might be playable. (It was no sure thing that Alou could catch it.)

In the ensuing days, Bartman stayed home from work, was castigated on the airwaves by broadcasters and fans, and in an additional statement noted that he and family members were subject to threats. He had offers to relocate to another state, which he declined, and received gifts from people and companies who felt sorry for his ordeal. Bartman indicated any goodies would be donated to the Juvenile Diabetes Research Foundation. That is the charity Ron Santo is linked with. Santo thanked Bartman and defended him as the "scapegoat" for the Cubs' bitter loss.

However, the storm had the staying power of Hurricane Katrina, and Bartman could do little but withstand the high winds. The gaffe occurred only a couple of weeks before Halloween and when the trick-or-treat holiday rolled around, joining the usual witches and ghosts on the street were a host of Bartmans, yep, decked out in baseball cap, headphones, and sweatshirt. The outfits were probably extra special hits in White Sox fan neighborhoods.

The Bartman developments rattled Cubs World. For once in their lives, Cubs fans thought they were on cruise control to the World Series. They had been a successful, popular team, seemingly with the right mix of players from Sosa to Prior to Kerry Wood to Alou. They did everything right for months, and then everything wrong for a moment, and with a little push from fate—after all, how else could you describe Bartman's intervention?—it all went poof. By the time the first pitch was thrown for the seventh game, Cubs fans harbored feelings of dread.

Of all the baseball poets and broadcasters, the anguished fans and players who commented on the goings-on, none summarized the season's highs and lows quite like Illinois U.S. Senator Dick Durbin. Franklin Adams lives. The Cubs of 2003 have their own sad lexicon.

On October 16, Durbin spoke in rhyme on the floor of the U.S. Senate, to "honor" the 2003 Cubs. He said in part:

There's weeping on Waveland
And Sheffield is dark,
Another sad ending
At Addison and Clark.
The Cubbies lost the big one
In the very last game,
A season so different
Has ended the same.
There's no Joy in Wrigleyville,
As the ivy turns brown,
But who can forget
The Cubs lit up the town.

And more:

Now in our despair
There's one thing to say,
Spring training is only
Four months away.
Next spring when the green
Is back on the vines,
Cubs fans will pour into
The Friendly Confines.
America, don't give up,
Don't falter, don't grieve,
If you wanna be a Cubs fan,
You gotta believe.

Robert Frost couldn't have put it any better.

If the season was dead, the ball took on a life of its own. The Bartman ball was taken home by a 33-year-old lawyer who later said he was selling it to raise money for a future child's college education. Harry Caray's Restaurant made the winning bid that, with taxes and fees factored in, cost nearly $114,000. The restaurant's managing partner Grant DePorter

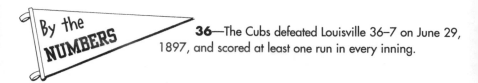

36—The Cubs defeated Louisville 36–7 on June 29, 1897, and scored at least one run in every inning.

said he was afraid the ball would fall into the hands of a Marlins fan. Presumably, that would leave Cubs fans subject to torment for the rest of their days, though the defeat to the eventual World Series champs seems to have done the trick.

DePorter announced the ball would be destroyed. One of the most amusing suggestions for obliteration was uttered by Dutchie Caray, the broadcaster's widow, who said, "How difficult is it going to be to cut up a baseball and fry it or something?"

But DePorter thought bigger than slicing and dicing. Using chemistry and special effects developed by experts, including an Academy Award–winner, the world's most famous foul ball was blown up on February 27, 2004, after the ball was served a last meal the night before. The execution was witnessed on national television at a tent set up outside the restaurant, and all proceeds from related activities were donated for juvenile diabetes research.

Dusty Baker, who still can't seem to comprehend all of the weirdness that surrounds Cubs history, said he was worried the stunt was just going to be wasteful. But he applauded the donation to charity.

"It's worth it then," Baker said.

When the ball went kablooey, master of ceremonies Tim Walkoe, a comedian, said, "You're now looking at $113,000 worth of string."

Bartman was invited to the blow-up but did not attend. In fact, Bartman has kept a low profile in Chicago since October 2003. He avoided TV cameras and talk shows. And now, unless he was dressed in a baseball cap, the same sweatshirt, and wearing headphones, it's doubtful anyone would recognize him walking down the street.

No More Lovable Losers and One Big Winner

Dusty Baker may have underestimated fate and curses, but he has instilled that "Why not us?" philosophy in the fans. Once content to absorb the atmosphere at their old ballpark, Cubs fans now harbor greater expectations.

Coming so close to the World Series in 2003, and starting 2004 as a favorite, even if injuries and a late September collapse ruined those hopes, have instilled a sense of entitlement in Cubs fans. Now they actually think the team can win it all, and the roster is stocked with players who understand that.

Greg Maddux did not return in the twilight of his career to play for a loser. Maddux, the one-time youthful star of the Cubs who won three Cy Young Awards and a World Series championship with the Atlanta Braves after winning his first Cy Young with the Cubs, returned to the fold in 2004 with the idea of rounding out a spectacular starting staff.

Maddux never possessed a supersonic fastball. His 6', 175-pound body never looked as if it had been constructed in the weight room. He was always deceptive. A righty with guile who was the best fielding pitcher of his generation, Maddux beat batters with location. He didn't overpower them, he fooled them. And he did it often enough to become what many say will be the last 300-game winner in major league history.

Downplaying his greatness with non-boastful remarks, Maddux, who would have listeners believe he's just an average Joe, achieved the 300-win milestone that has measured top pitchers throughout the decades with an 8–4 victory over the San Francisco Giants on August 7, 2004.

A year later, on July 26, Maddux became the 14th pitcher in major league history to strike out 3,000 batters and only the ninth to have both 300 wins and 3,000 K's on his résumé.

Maddux, whose competitiveness as much as his fastball set him apart, said he was happy to record the big strikeout of Omar Vizquel of the Giants at Wrigley, but in typical fashion said he did not want it to become bigger than the team's doings.

"You never want anything to take away from what the team's trying to accomplish," he said. "I don't try to strike guys out. I never have. I've always tried to just make a pitch, but I found myself trying to strike somebody out and it took me out of my game a little bit. It was pretty cool pitching on the mound with that [crowd noise]. You hear it. believe me, you hear it. The fans here are super."

Maddux, who ended the 2005 season with 318 victories, said it was possible that he might retire, but Baker swiftly noted that Maddux would be welcome back and Maddux met the criteria in his contract for another $8 million year with the Cubs. On a team that finished under .500 for the first time in three seasons under Baker, Maddux was far from the biggest worry. On a team that figured to be healthier, Maddux seemed to have one more run at glory in his arm.

Maddux' main off-field obsession is probably golf, and that is a sport he can play for decades once he rests his arm.

One of the remarkable things about the Cubs is how successful they are at the gate, drawing millions of fans even when the team has no chance to win a pennant. Illustrating the uniqueness of the franchise and the fans who back it, was the creation of the theatrical play *Bleacher Bums*, first staged in 1977. The endearing show is as much about the people who live for the Cubs as the Cubs themselves, and was a poignant and popular play.

Showing that some things never change—at least the Cubs' image as lovable losers—the show, which over the years starred Joe Mantegna, Dennis Franz, George Wendt, and Charles Durning, among others, bounced back again in 2004. While neither the fans nor players might be so easily classified as bums anymore, the story is reasonably timeless. And since the Cubs still hadn't won a World Series, a revival seemed appropriate.

TOP TEN

Cubs Single-Season Win Percentage (since 1900)

	Name	Year	Record	Win Percentage
1.	Rick Sutcliffe	1984	16–1	.941
2.	Hank Borowy	1945	11–2	.846
3.	Leonard Cole	1910	20–4	.833
4.	Ed Reulbach	1906	19–4	.826
5.	Mordecai "Three Finger" Brown	1906	26–6	.813
6.	Ed Reulbach	1907	17–4	.810
7.	Orval Overall	1906	12–3	.800 t
	Jack Taylor	1906	12–3	.800 t
9.	Bert Humphries	1913	16–4	.800
10.	Lon Warneke	1932	22–6	.786

Some things never change on the North Side. Nationally, the Cubs have often been compared to the Boston Red Sox as teams with long-suffering fans. The Red Sox broke their own curse, dispatching the St. Louis Cardinals to win the 2004 World Series. Still, the clubs remain linked in the public eye because they play in the two oldest ballparks in captivity. The Cubs have Wrigley, the Red Sox have Fenway, and both teams have rabid, long-time fans.

Todd Walker has played second base for both clubs, currently the Cubs, and he said the teams and their parks are in a league of their own.

"They're both the best ballparks in the country," Walker said. "There's no other parks that compare to these two. The fans are very similar, very knowledgeable, very passionate, and the cities are great, as well. When they tore down Tiger Stadium, and places like that, I would rather have seen them just renovate. I think a lot of our sport lives off the history. I think that's why Wrigley and Fenway do so well—because of the history.

"The players don't talk about them while they're playing, but in the end it's fun to say that you've played in those parks."

It's even more fun to win in those parks and, alas, generations of Cubs players have not had that thrill.

"It's unfortunate that I didn't get to a World Series," said Ernie Banks. "My World Series was winning the respect of the fans, the media, and my family. That and building friendships. That's what counts, things that will last."

The Cubs have become a national phenomenon. When they travel it is not uncommon for ballparks to hold as many fans as the home team gets.

TRIVIA

What are the Chicago Cubs' minor league affiliates?

Answers to the trivia questions are on pages 158–159.

"They live and die with it like we do," said Cubs pitcher Michael Wuertz. "It's great to have fans who have as much invested as we do. We were in San Diego and half the crowd was Cubs fans. There are Cubs fans everywhere."

Nomar Garciaparra, who moved from one historic franchise to another when he was traded from the Red Sox to the Cubs, said the road support can be overwhelming.

"There are places where it feels like a home game," Garciaparra said.

The Cubs' season of 2005 was a major letdown. Injuries and surprisingly bland performances in many cases exiled the team to also-ran status with two months to go. Although Derrek Lee put together one of the best Cubs seasons in home runs (46), RBIs (107), and average (.335 to lead the league), the true highlight of the summer was the induction of second baseman Ryne Sandberg into the Hall of Fame at the end of July.

Sandberg made it to the majors with Philadelphia in 1981 and after a trade stuck with the Cubs until 1997, although he did take a year off for personal reasons. Sandberg was a slick fielder of second-base stereotype, who also combined surprising power, a rarity at the position. Sandberg won nine Gold Glove awards while setting the major league record of .989 for career fielding percentage at his position, made the All-Star team 10 times, had a .285 lifetime average, and, at the time of his retirement, held the record for home runs by a second baseman (277 of his career 282). He was the Most Valuable Player of the 1984 season.

The slugging second baseman also had one game that defined his greatness at bat. In Cubs World it is called simply the "Ryne Sandberg Game." Players and fans alike refer to it that way.

When Dusty Baker was hired as manager of the Cubs in 2002, he immediately began talking about helping the team to its first world championship since 1908. "Why not us?" Baker said.

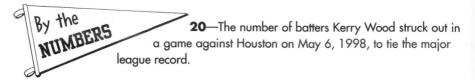

20—The number of batters Kerry Wood struck out in a game against Houston on May 6, 1998, to tie the major league record.

Sandberg carried the Cubs to a dramatic, nationally televised triumph over their fierce St. Louis rival. Sandberg not only hit two home runs and swatted three singles to drive in seven runs, some of the mystique surrounds the timing and circumstances of his big hits, beating the Cardinals in extra innings.

Many years later, Sandberg said when he meets people they bring up that performance.

"Everyone tells me where they were when they watched that game," he said.

Cardinals manager Whitey Herzog said Sandberg was the best player he had ever seen and called him "Baby Ruth."

Sandberg may not always have been Ruthian at the plate, but he joined the Bambino in the Hall of Fame with a remarkable speech at his induction ceremony in Cooperstown, New York, on July 31, 2005. At a time when baseball was under pressure from Congress and public opinion to clean up its ways and crack down harder on steroid users and drug cheats, Sandberg, then 45, spoke from the heart about the game he loves.

In a 23-minute speech lauded coast-to-coast, Sandberg criticized players who show the game no respect and who demonstrate selfishness on the diamond.

"I stand here today before you humbled, and a grateful baseball player," Sandberg began.

"The game fit me because it was all about doing things right. If you played the game the right way, played the game for the team, good things would happen.

"I was taught you never, ever disrespect your opponent, or your teammates, or your organization, or your manager, and never, ever your uniform."

When Sandberg finished talking in Cooperstown, the applause was deafening. When Sandberg came home to Wrigley Field on August 28 to have his No. 23 uniform jersey retired, the applause was even louder.

There was a sweetness and a sadness in the air—sweetness because the emotion on display was all about respect for the way Sandberg played the game; sadness because he is retired, will no longer field those ground balls with alacrity and confidence, and because he will not be playing when the Cubs chase down that elusive world championship to bookend the one captured nearly a century ago.

Chances are that the great third baseman Ron Santo will be around to call it, however, if it comes to pass anytime soon.

"I feel like Cub fans," Santo said. "I truly, truly believe this, and you know everybody laughs—wait till next year. The real truth is that Cubs fans believe in next year."

Answers to
Trivia Questions

Page 3: Larry Corcoran defeated the Boston Braves 6–0 on August 19, 1880.

Page 29: Yes. Outfielder Gary Woods fielded flawlessly in 103 games in 1982, and outfielder Doug Dascenzo did so also in 107 games in 1990.

Page 30: When right fielder Frank "Wildfire" Schulte was declared the most valuable player in the National League in 1911, it was called the Chalmers Award.

Page 36: The Cubs began wearing numbers on the back of their uniforms during the 1932 season.

Page 41: Multitalented actor Chuck Connors, who starred in The Rifleman on television, played for the Cubs.

Page 43: From their creation in 1876 until the 1940s, the Cubs never had a losing record across a decade. Although the team won the 1945 pennant—its most recent—the World War II period was marked by repeated losing seasons.

Page 52: It's not even close. Adrian "Cap" Anson, player/manager for much of his association with the Cubs, won 1,283 games at the helm, managing between 1879 and 1897.

Page 61: Mordecai "Three Finger" Brown recorded a 1.04 earned-run average in 1906.

Page 71: Interim manager Bruce Kimm, who had a record of 33–45 to close out the 2002 season.

Page 77: Jon Lieber, May 24, against Cincinnati, and Kerry Wood, May 25, 2001, against Milwaukee.

Page 93: Four. Ferguson Jenkins in 1971, Bruce Sutter in 1979, Rick Sutcliffe in 1984, and Greg Maddux in 1992.

Page 100: Twenty, in 1902. There were so many young players that season—as in baby bears—that it helped transform the team nickname to "Cubs" for good.

Page 109: Bill Madlock, who in 1975 shared the MVP award with Mets pitcher Jon Matlack. Madlock's two-run, ninth-inning single won the game for the National League.

Page 112: Billy Williams, 1961; Ken Hubbs, 1962; Jerome Walton, 1989; Kerry Wood, 1998.

Page 127: Charlie Grimm in 1936 and 1946; Gabby Hartnett in 1939; and Dusty Baker in 2003.

ANSWERS TO TRIVIA QUESTIONS

Page 132: Bill Madlock led the league in hitting with a .354 average in 1975 and won the batting title again in 1976 with a .339 average.

Page 135: As of the end of the 2005 season, Dusty Baker ranked fifth among active managers in wins, behind Tony LaRussa, Bobby Cox, Joe Torre, and Lou Piniella.

Page 143: Rogers Hornsby, with 229 base hits in 1929.

Page 154: Iowa Cubs (Triple A), West Tennessee Diamond Jaxx (Double A), Daytona Cubs (A), Peoria Chiefs (A), Boise Hawks (short-season A), Mesa Cubs (rookie), Dominican Cubs (rookie).

Chicago Cubs
All-Time Roster

Players who have appeared in at least one game with the Chicago Cubs

* Player still active in Major League Baseball.

A

David Aardsma*	Pitcher	2005
Bert Abbey	Pitcher	1893–95
Ted Abernathy	Pitcher	1965–66, 1969–70
Cliff Aberson	Outfielder	1947–49
Johnny Abrego	Pitcher	1985
Jimmy Adair	Shortstop	1931
Bobby Adams	Third Base	1957–59
Karl Adams	Pitcher	1915
Mike Adams	Outfielder	1976–77
Red Adams	Pitcher	1946
Sparky Adams	Second Base	1922–27
Terry Adams*	Pitcher	1995–99
Bob Addis	Outfielder	1952–53
Bob Addy	Outfielder	1876
Dewey Adkins	Pitcher	1949
Rick Aguilera	Pitcher	1999–2000
Hank Aguirre	Pitcher	1969–70
Jack Aker	Pitcher	1972–73
Dale Alderson	Pitcher	1943–44
Vic Aldridge	Pitcher	1917–18, 1922–24
Grover Alexander	Pitcher	1918–26
Manny Alexander*	Shortstop	1997–99
Matt Alexander	Outfielder	1973–74
Antonio Alfonseca*	Pitcher	2002–03
Ethan Allen	Outfielder	1936
Nick Allen	Catcher	1916
Milo Allison	Outfielder	1913–14
Moises Alou*	Outfielder	2002–04
Porfi Altamirano	Pitcher	1984
George Altman	Outfielder	1959–62, 1965–67
Joey Amalfitano	Second Base	1964–67
Vicente Amor	Pitcher	1955
Bob Anderson	Pitcher	1957–62
Jimmy Anderson*	Pitcher	2004
John Andre	Pitcher	1955
Jim Andrews	Outfielder	1890
Shane Andrews	Third Base	1999–2000
Fred Andrus	Outfielder	1876, 1884
Tom Angley	Catcher	1929
Cap Anson	First Base	1876–97
Jimmy Archer	Catcher	1909–17
Jose Arcia	Shortstop	1968
Alex Arias*	Shortstop	1992
Jamie Arnold	Pitcher	2000
Jim Asbell	Outfielder	1938
Richie Ashburn	Outfielder	1960–61
Ken Aspromonte	Second Base	1963
Paul Assenmacher	Pitcher	1989–93
Toby Atwell	Catcher	1952–53
Earl Averill	Catcher	1959–60
Bobby Ayala	Pitcher	1999
Manny Aybar*	Pitcher	2001

B

Fred Baczewski	Pitcher	1953
Ed Baecht	Pitcher	1931–32
Ed Bailey	Catcher	1965
Sweetbreads Bailey	Pitcher	1919–21
Gene Baker	Second Base	1953–57
Tom Baker	Pitcher	1963
Paul Bako*	Catcher	2003–04
Mark Baldwin	Pitcher	1887–88
Jay Baller	Pitcher	1985–87
Tony Balsamo	Pitcher	1962
Ernie Banks	First Base	1953–71
Willie Banks*	Pitcher	1994–95
Steve Barber	Pitcher	1970
Turner Barber	Outfielder	1917–22
Bret Barberie	Second Base	1996
Richard Barker	Pitcher	1999
Ross Barnes	Second Base	1876–77
Cuno Barragan	Catcher	1961–63
Bob Barrett	Third Base	1923–25
Dick Barrett	Pitcher	1943
Michael Barrett*	Catcher	2004–05
Shad Barry	Outfielder	1904–05
Dick Bartell	Shortstop	1939
Vince Barton	Outfielder	1931–32
Cliff Bartosh*	Pitcher	2005
Charlie Bastian	Shortstop	1889
Johnny Bates	Outfielder	1914
Miguel Batista*	Pitcher	1997
Allen Battle	Outfielder	1998–99
Russ Bauers	Pitcher	1946
Frank Baumann	Pitcher	1965
Frank Baumholtz	Outfielder	1949, 1951–55
Jose Bautista	Pitcher	1993–94
Tommy Beals	Outfielder	1880
Dave Beard	Pitcher	1985
Ginger Beaumont	Outfielder	1910
Clyde Beck	Third Base	1926–30
Rod Beck*	Pitcher	1998–99
Heinz Becker	First Base	1943, 1945–46
Glenn Beckert	Second Base	1965–73
Fred Beebe	Pitcher	1906

George Bell	Outfielder	1991
Les Bell	Third Base	1930–31
Mark Bellhorn*	Second Base	2002–03
Francis Beltran*	Pitcher	2002, 2004
Alan Benes*	Pitcher	2002–03
Butch Benton	Catcher	1982
Jason Bere	Pitcher	2001–02
Justin Berg*	Pitcher	2005
Joe Berry	Pitcher	1942
Damon Berryhill	Catcher	1987–91
Dick Bertell	Catcher	1960–65, 1967
Oscar Bielaski	Outfielder	1875–76
Mike Bielecki	Pitcher	1988–91
Larry Biittner	Outfielder	1976–80
Steve Bilko	First Base	1954
Doug Bird	Pitcher	1981–82
Bill Bishop	Pitcher	1889
Hi Bithorn	Pitcher	1942–43, 1946
Earl Blackburn	Catcher	1917
Tim Blackwell	Catcher	1978–81
Rick Bladt	Outfielder	1969
Footsie Blair	Second Base	1929–31
Sheriff Blake	Pitcher	1924–31
Henry Blanco*	Catcher	2005
Kevin Blankenship	Pitcher	1988–90
Jeff Blauser	Shortstop	1998–99
Cy Block	Third Base	1942, 1945–46
Randy Bobb	Catcher	1968–69
John Boccabella	Catcher	1963–68
Jim Bolger	Outfielder	1955, 1957–58
Bobby Bonds	Outfielder	1981
Julio Bonetti	Pitcher	1940
Bill Bonham	Pitcher	1971–77
Zeke Bonura	First Base	1940
George Borchers	Pitcher	1888
Rich Bordi	Pitcher	1983–84
Bob Borkowski	Outfielder	1950–51
Steve Boros	Third Base	1963
Joe Borowski*	Pitcher	2001–05
Hank Borowy	Pitcher	1945–48

Shawn Boskie	Pitcher	1990–94		Lew Brown	Catcher	1879
Thad Bosley	Outfielder	1983–86		Mordecai Brown	Pitcher	1904–12, 1916
Derek Botelho	Pitcher	1985		Ray Brown	Pitcher	1909
John Bottarini	Catcher	1937		Roosevelt Brown*	Outfielder	1999–2002
Kent Bottenfield	Pitcher	1996–97		Tommy Brown	Shortstop	1952–53
Ed Bouchee	First Base	1960–61		Byron Browne	Outfielder	1965–67
Pat Bourque	First Base	1971–73		George Browne	Outfielder	1909
Larry Bowa	Shortstop	1982–85		Mike Brumley	Shortstop	1987
Micah Bowie*	Pitcher	1999		Warren Brusstar	Pitcher	1983–85
Bill Bowman	Catcher	1891		Clay Bryant	Pitcher	1935–40
Bob Bowman	Pitcher	1942		Don Bryant	Catcher	1966
Bill Bradley	Third Base	1899–1900		Tod Brynan	Pitcher	1888
George Bradley	Pitcher	1877		Bill Buckner	First Base	1977–84
Spike Brady	Outfielder	1875		Steve Buechele	Third Base	1992–95
Mike Brannock	Third Base	1875		Art Bues	Third Base	1914
Kitty Bransfield	First Base	1911		Damon Buford	Outfielder	2000–01
Danny Breeden	Catcher	1971		Bob Buhl	Pitcher	1962–66
Hal Breeden	First Base	1971		Scott Bullett*	Outfielder	1995–96
William Brennan	Pitcher	1993		Jim Bullinger*	Pitcher	1992–96
Roger Bresnahan	Catcher	1900, 1913–15		Freddie Burdette	Pitcher	1962–64
Herb Brett	Pitcher	1924–25		Lew Burdette	Pitcher	1964–65
Jim Brewer	Pitcher	1960–63		Smoky Burgess	Catcher	1949, 1951
Charlie Brewster	Shortstop	1944		Leo Burke	Outfielder	1963–65
Al Bridwell	Shortstop	1913		Jeromy Burnitz*	Outfielder	2005
Buttons Briggs	Pitcher	1896–98, 1904–05		Tom Burns	Third Base	1880–91
Dan Briggs	First Base	1982		Ray Burris	Pitcher	1973–79
John Briggs	Pitcher	1956–58		John Burrows	Pitcher	1943–44
Harry Bright	First Base	1965		Ellis Burton	Outfielder	1963–65
Jim Brillheart	Pitcher	1927		Dick Burwell	Pitcher	1960–61
Leon Brinkopf	Shortstop	1952		Guy Bush	Pitcher	1923–34
Pete Broberg	Pitcher	1977		Johnny Butler	Shortstop	1928
Lou Brock	Outfielder	1961–64		John Buzhardt	Pitcher	1958–59
Tarrik Brock	Outfielder	2000				
Ernie Broglio	Pitcher	1964–66		**C**		
Herman Bronkie	Third Base	1914		Miguel Cairo*	Second Base	1997, 2001
Mandy Brooks	Outfielder	1925–26		Marty Callaghan	Outfielder	1922–23
Jim Brosnan	Pitcher	1954, 1956–58		Nixey Callahan	Outfielder	1897–00
Brant Brown	Outfielder	1996–98, 2000		Johnny Callison	Outfielder	1970–71
Joe Brown	Pitcher	1884		Dick Calmus	Pitcher	1967
Jophery Brown	Pitcher	1968		Dolph Camilli	First Base	1933–34
Jumbo Brown	Pitcher	1925		Kid Camp	Pitcher	1894

Lew Camp	Third Base	1893–94	Cupid Childs	Second Base	1900–01
Bill Campbell	Pitcher	1982–83	Pete Childs	Second Base	1901
Gilly Campbell	Catcher	1933	Bob Chipman	Pitcher	1944–49
Joe Campbell	Outfielder	1967	Harry Chiti	Catcher	1950–52, 1955–56
Mike Campbell	Pitcher	1996	Hee–Seop Choi*	First Base	2002–03
Ron Campbell	Second Base	1964–66	Steve Christmas	Catcher	1986
Vin Campbell	Outfielder	1908	Loyd Christopher	Outfielder	1945
Jim Canavan	Outfielder	1892	Bubba Church	Pitcher	1953–55
Robinson Cancel*	Catcher	2005	Len Church	Pitcher	1966
Chris Cannizzaro	Catcher	1971	John Churry	Catcher	1924–27
Mike Capel	Pitcher	1988	Dad Clark	First Base	1902
Doug Capilla	Pitcher	1979–81	Dave Clark	Outfielder	1990, 1997
Jose Cardenal	Outfielder	1972–77	Mark Clark	Pitcher	1997–98
Don Cardwell	Pitcher	1960–62	Dad Clarke	Pitcher	1888
Tex Carleton	Pitcher	1935–38	Henry Clarke	Pitcher	1898
Don Carlsen	Pitcher	1948	Sumpter Clarke	Outfielder	1920
Hal Carlson	Pitcher	1927–30	Tommy Clarke	Catcher	1918
Bill Carney	Outfielder	1904	John Clarkson	Pitcher	1884–87
Bob Carpenter	Pitcher	1947	Fritz Clausen	Pitcher	1893–94
Cliff Carroll	Outfielder	1890–91	Clem Clemens	Catcher	1916
Al Carson	Pitcher	1910	Doug Clemens	Outfielder	1964–65
Joe Carter	Outfielder	1983	Matt Clement*	Pitcher	2002–04
Paul Carter	Pitcher	1916–20	Ty Cline	Outfielder	1966
Rico Carty	Outfielder	1973	Gene Clines	Outfielder	1977–79
Bob Caruthers	Outfielder	1893	Billy Clingman	Third Base	1900
Doc Casey	Third Base	1903–05	Otis Clymer	Outfielder	1913
Hugh Casey	Pitcher	1935	Andy Coakley	Pitcher	1908–09
Larry Casian	Pitcher	1995–97	Kevin Coffman	Pitcher	1990
John Cassidy	Outfielder	1878	Dick Cogan	Pitcher	1899
Frank Castillo*	Pitcher	1991–97	Frank Coggins	Second Base	1972
Bill Caudill	Pitcher	1979–81	Hy Cohen	Pitcher	1955
Phil Cavarretta	First Base	1934–53	Jim Colborn	Pitcher	1969–71
Art Ceccarelli	Pitcher	1959–60	Dave Cole	Pitcher	1954
Ronny Cedeno*	Shortstop	2005	King Cole	Pitcher	1909–12
Ron Cey	Third Base	1983–86	Joe Coleman	Pitcher	1976
Cliff Chambers	Pitcher	1948	Bill Collins	Outfielder	1911
Frank Chance	First Base	1898–12	Dan Collins	Outfielder	1874
Harry Chapman	Catcher	1912	Phil Collins	Pitcher	1923
Virgil Cheeves	Pitcher	1920–23	Rip Collins	Catcher	1940
Larry Cheney	Pitcher	1911–15	Ripper Collins	First Base	1937–38
Scott Chiasson*	Pitcher	2001–02	Jackie Collum	Pitcher	1957

Jorge Comellas	Pitcher	1945		Doc Curley	Second Base	1899
Clint Compton	Pitcher	1972		Clarence Currie	Pitcher	1903
Bunk Congalton	Outfielder	1902		Cliff Curtis	Pitcher	1911
Fritzie Connally	Third Base	1983		Jack Curtis	Pitcher	1961–62
Terry Connell	Catcher	1874		Jack Cusick	Shortstop	1951
Jim Connor	Second Base	1892, 1897–99		Ned Cuthbert	Outfielder	1874
Bill Connors	Pitcher	1966		Kiki Cuyler	Outfielder	1928–35
Chuck Connors	First Base	1951		Mike Cvengros	Pitcher	1929
Jim Cook	Outfielder	1903				
Ron Coomer*	First Base	2001		**D**		
Jimmy Cooney	Shortstop	1890–92		Bill Dahlen	Shortstop	1891–98
Jimmy Cooney	Shortstop	1926–27		Babe Dahlgren	First Base	1941–42
Mort Cooper	Pitcher	1949		Con Daily	Catcher	1896
Walker Cooper	Catcher	1954–55		Dom Dallessandro	Outfielder	1940–44,
Wilbur Cooper	Pitcher	1925–26				1946–47
Larry Corcoran	Pitcher	1880–85		Abner Dalrymple	Outfielder	1879–86
Mike Corcoran	Pitcher	1884		Tom Daly	Second Base	1887–88
Red Corriden	Shortstop	1913–15		Tom Daly	Catcher	1918–21
Frank Corridon	Pitcher	1904		Kal Daniels	Outfielder	1992
Jim Cosman	Pitcher	1970		Alvin Dark	Shortstop	1958–59
Dick Cotter	Catcher	1912		Dell Darling	Catcher	1887–89
Hooks Cotter	First Base	1922, 1924		Bobby Darwin	Outfielder	1977
Henry Cotto	Outfielder	1984		Doug Dascenzo	Outfielder	1988–92
Ensign Cottrell	Pitcher	1912		Bill Davidson	Outfielder	1909
Roscoe Coughlin	Pitcher	1890		Brock Davis	Outfielder	1970–71
Wes Covington	Outfielder	1966		Curt Davis	Pitcher	1936–37
Billy Cowan	Outfielder	1963–64		Jim Davis	Pitcher	1954–56
Larry Cox	Catcher	1978, 1982		Jody Davis	Catcher	1981–88
Doug Creek*	Pitcher	1999		Ron Davis	Pitcher	1986–87
Chuck Crim	Pitcher	1994		Steve Davis	Second Base	1979
Harry Croft	Outfielder	1901		Tommy Davis	Outfielder	1970, 1972
George Crosby	Pitcher	1884		Gookie Dawkins*	Shortstop	2004
Ken Crosby	Pitcher	1975–76		Andre Dawson	Outfielder	1987–92
Jeff Cross	Shortstop	1948		Boots Day	Outfielder	1970
Dave Crouthers	Pitcher	2005		Brian Dayett	Outfielder	1985–87
Juan Cruz*	Pitcher	2001–03		Ivan DeJesus	Shortstop	1977–81
Hector Cruz	Outfielder	1978, 1981–82		Delino DeShields	Second Base	2001–02
Dick Culler	Shortstop	1948		Charlie Deal	Third Base	1916–21
Ray Culp	Pitcher	1967		Dizzy Dean	Pitcher	1938–41
Will Cunnane*	Pitcher	2002		Wayland Dean	Pitcher	1927
Bert Cunningham	Pitcher	1900–01		George Decker	Outfielder	1892–97

Joe Decker	Pitcher	1969–72	Red Downs	Second Base	1912
Jim Delahanty	Second Base	1901	Scott Downs*	Pitcher	2000
Bobby Delgreco	Outfielder	1957	Jack Doyle	First Base	1901
Fred Demarais	Pitcher	1890	Jim Doyle	Third Base	1911
Al Demaree	Pitcher	1917	Larry Doyle	Second Base	1916–17
Frank Demaree	Outfielder	1932–33, 1935–38	Moe Drabowsky	Pitcher	1956–60
			Sammy Drake	Second Base	1960–61
Harry Demiller	Pitcher	1892	Solly Drake	Outfielder	1956
Gene Demontreville	Second Base	1899	Paddy Driscoll	Second Base	1917
Ryan Dempster*	Pitcher	2004–05	Dick Drott	Pitcher	1957–61
Roger Denzer	Pitcher	1897	Monk Dubiel	Pitcher	1949–52
Bob Dernier	Outfielder	1984–87	Jason Dubois*	Outfielder	2004–05
Claud Derrick	Shortstop	1914	Hugh Duffy	Outfielder	1888–89
Paul Derringer	Pitcher	1943–45	Nick Dumovich	Pitcher	1923
Tom Dettore	Pitcher	1974–76	Courtney Duncan*	Pitcher	2001–02
Jim Devlin	Pitcher	1874–75	Jim Dunegan	Pitcher	1970
Charlie Dexter	Outfielder	1900–02	Sam Dungan	Outfielder	1892–94, 1900
Mike DiFelice*	Catcher	2004	Ron Dunn	Second Base	1974–75
Mike Diaz	First Base	1983	Shawon Dunston	Shortstop	1985–95, 1997
Lance Dickson	Pitcher	1990	Todd Dunwoody*	Outfielder	2001
Steve Dillard	Second Base	1979–81	Kid Durbin	Outfielder	1907–08
Pickles Dillhoefer	Catcher	1917	Leon Durham	First Base	1981–88
Miguel Dilone	Outfielder	1979	Frank Dwyer	Pitcher	1888–89
Frank Dipino	Pitcher	1986–88			
Alec Distaso	Pitcher	1969	**E**		
John Dobbs	Outfielder	1902–03	Don Eaddy	Third Base	1959
Jess Dobernic	Pitcher	1948–49	Bill Eagan	Second Base	1893
Cozy Dolan	Outfielder	1900–01	Howard Earl	Outfielder	1890
John Dolan	Pitcher	1895	Arnold Earley	Pitcher	1966
Tom Dolan	Catcher	1879	Mal Eason	Pitcher	1900–02
Tim Donahue	Catcher	1895–1900	Roy Easterwood	Catcher	1944
Ed Donnelly	Pitcher	1959	Rawly Eastwick	Pitcher	1981
Frank Donnelly	Pitcher	1893	Vallie Eaves	Pitcher	1941–42
Mickey Doolan	Shortstop	1916	Angel Echevarria*	Outfielder	2002
Brian Dorsett	Catcher	1996	Eric Eckenstahler*	Pitcher	2004
Herm Doscher	Third Base	1879	Dennis Eckersley	Pitcher	1984–86
Jack Doscher	Pitcher	1903	Charlie Eden	Outfielder	1877
Phil Douglas	Pitcher	1915, 1917–19	Tom Edens	Pitcher	1995
Taylor Douthit	Outfielder	1933	Bruce Edwards	Catcher	1951–52, 1954
Dave Dowling	Pitcher	1966	Hank Edwards	Outfielder	1949–50
Tom Downey	Shortstop	1912	Dave Eggler	Outfielder	1877

Ed Eiteljorge	Pitcher	1890	William Fischer	Catcher	1916
Lee Elia	Shortstop	1968	Bob Fisher	Shortstop	1914–15
Pete Elko	Third Base	1943–44	Cherokee Fisher	Pitcher	1877
Allen Elliott	First Base	1923–24	Howie Fitzgerald	Outfielder	1922, 1924
Carter Elliott	Shortstop	1921	Max Flack	Outfielder	1916–22
Rowdy Elliott	Catcher	1916–18	John Flavin	Pitcher	1964
Jim Ellis	Pitcher	1967	Bill Fleming	Pitcher	1942–44, 1946
Dick Ellsworth	Pitcher	1958, 1960–66	Scott Fletcher	Shortstop	1981–82
Don Elston	Pitcher	1953, 1957–64	Silver Flint	Catcher	1879–89
Mario Encarnacion	Outfielder	2002	Jesse Flores	Pitcher	1942
Steve Engel	Pitcher	1985	John Fluhrer	Outfielder	1915
Woody English	Shortstop	1927–36	George Flynn	Outfielder	1896
Al Epperly	Pitcher	1938	Jocko Flynn	Pitcher	1886–87
Paul Erickson	Pitcher	1941–48	Gene Fodge	Pitcher	1958
Frank Ernaga	Outfielder	1957–58	Will Foley	Third Base	1875
Dick Errickson	Pitcher	1942	Dee Fondy	First Base	1951–57
Shawn Estes*	Pitcher	2003	Mike Fontenot*	Second Base	2005
Chuck Estrada	Pitcher	1966	Ray Fontenot	Pitcher	1985–86
Uel Eubanks	Pitcher	1922	Barry Foote	Catcher	1979–81
Bill Everitt	First Base	1895–1900	Davy Force	Shortstop	1874
Johnny Evers	Second Base	1902–13	Tony Fossas	Pitcher	1998
Scott Eyre*	Pitcher	2005	Elmer Foster	Outfielder	1890–91
			Kevin Foster*	Pitcher	1994–98
F			Chad Fox*	Pitcher	2005
Jim Fanning	Catcher	1954–57	Bill Foxen	Pitcher	1910–11
Carmen Fanzone	Third Base	1971–74	Jimmie Foxx	First Base	1942, 1944
Kyle Farnsworth*	Pitcher	1999–04	Ken Frailing	Pitcher	1974–76
Doc Farrell	Shortstop	1930	Ossie France	Pitcher	1890
Duke Farrell	Catcher	1888–89	Matt Franco*	First Base	1995
Jeff Fassero*	Pitcher	2001–02	Terry Francona	First Base	1986
Darcy Fast	Pitcher	1968	Chick Fraser	Pitcher	1907–09
Bill Faul	Pitcher	1965–66	George Frazier	Pitcher	1984–86
Vern Fear	Pitcher	1952	Buck Freeman	Pitcher	1921–22
Marv Felderman	Catcher	1942	Hersh Freeman	Pitcher	1958
John Felske	Catcher	1968	Mark Freeman	Pitcher	1960
Bob Ferguson	Third Base	1878	George Freese	Third Base	1961
Charlie Ferguson	Pitcher	1901	Howard Freigau	Third Base	1925–27
Felix Fermin	Shortstop	1996	Larry French	Pitcher	1935–41
Frank Fernandez	Catcher	1971–72	Lonny Frey	Second Base	1937, 1947
Jesus Figueroa	Outfielder	1980	Bernie Friberg	Third Base	1919–20,
Tom Filer	Pitcher	1982			1922–25

Danny Friend	Pitcher	1895–98	Norm Gigon	Second Base	1967
Owen Friend	Second Base	1955–56	Charlie Gilbert	Outfielder	1941–43, 1946
Woodie Fryman	Pitcher	1978	Johnny Gill	Outfielder	1935–36
Oscar Fuhr	Pitcher	1921	Paul Gillespie	Catcher	1942, 1944–45
Fred Fussell	Pitcher	1922–23	— Gilroy	Catcher	1874
Mike Fyhrie*	Pitcher	2001	Joe Girardi	Catcher	1989–92, 2000–02

G

			Dave Giusti	Pitcher	1977
Gabe Gabler	--	1958	Fred Glade	Pitcher	1902
Len Gabrielson	Outfielder	1964–65	Doug Glanville*	Outfielder	1996–97, 2003
Gary Gaetti	Third Base	1998–99	Jim Gleeson	Outfielder	1939–40
Phil Gagliano	Second Base	1970	Bob Glenalvin	Second Base	1890, 1893
Steve Gajkowski	Pitcher	1998–99	Ed Glenn	Shortstop	1902
Augie Galan	Outfielder	1934–41	John Glenn	Outfielder	1874–77
Oscar Gamble	Outfielder	1969	Ross Gload*	First Base	2000
Bill Gannon	Outfielder	1901	Al Glossop	Second Base	1946
John Ganzel	First Base	1900	John Goetz	Pitcher	1960
Joe Garagiola	Catcher	1953–54	Mike Golden	Outfielder	1875
Bob Garbark	Catcher	1937–39	Fred Goldsmith	Pitcher	1880–84
Rich Garces*	Pitcher	1995	Walt Golvin	First Base	1922
Nomar Garciaparra*	Shortstop	2004–05	Leo Gomez	Third Base	1996
Jim Gardner	Pitcher	1902	Alex Gonzalez*	Shortstop	2002–04
Rob Gardner	Pitcher	1967	Jeremi Gonzalez*	Pitcher	1997–98
Daniel Garibay	Pitcher	2000	Luis Gonzalez*	Outfielder	1995–96
Mike Garman	Pitcher	1976	Mike Gonzalez	Catcher	1925–29
Adrian Garrett	Designated Hitter	1970, 1973–75	Raul Gonzalez*	Outfielder	2000
			Wilbur Good	Outfielder	1911–15
Cecil Garriott	--	1946	Ival Goodman	Outfielder	1943–44
Ned Garvin	Pitcher	1899–1900	Curtis Goodwin	Outfielder	1999
Charlie Gassaway	Pitcher	1944	Tom Goodwin*	Outfielder	2003–04
Ed Gastfield	Catcher	1885	Mike Gordon	Catcher	1977–78
Chippy Gaw	Pitcher	1920	Tom Gordon*	Pitcher	2001–02
Dave Geisel	Pitcher	1978–79, 1981	George Gore	Outfielder	1879–86
Emil Geiss	Pitcher	1887	Hank Gornicki	Pitcher	1941
Greek George	Catcher	1941	Johnny Goryl	Second Base	1957–59
Dave Gerard	Pitcher	1962	Rich Gossage	Pitcher	1988
George Gerberman	Pitcher	1962	Billy Grabarkewitz	Third Base	1974
Dick Gernert	First Base	1960	Earl Grace	Catcher	1929, 1931
Jody Gerut*	Outfielder	2005	Mark Grace	First Base	1988–2000
Doc Gessler	Outfielder	1906	Peaches Graham	Catcher	1903, 1911
Robert Gibson	Pitcher	1890	Alex Grammas	Shortstop	1962–63

Hank Grampp	Pitcher	1927, 1929
Tom Grant	Outfielder	1983
George Grantham	Second Base	1922–24
Joe Graves	Third Base	1926
Danny Green	Outfielder	1898–1901
Scarborough Green*	Outfielder	2000–01
Adam Greenberg*	Outfielder	2005
Willie Greene	Third Base	2000
Lee Gregory	Pitcher	1964
Ben Grieve*	Outfielder	2004–05
Hank Griffin	Pitcher	1911
Mike Griffin	Pitcher	1981
Clark Griffith	Pitcher	1893–1900
Frank Griffith	Pitcher	1892
Tommy Griffith	Outfielder	1925
Denver Grigsby	Outfielder	1923–25
Burleigh Grimes	Pitcher	1932–33
Ray Grimes	First Base	1921–24
Charlie Grimm	First Base	1925–36
Greg Gross	Outfielder	1977–78
Ernie Groth	Pitcher	1904
Mark Grudzielanek*	Second Base	2003–04
Marv Gudat	Outfielder	1932
Ad Gumbert	Pitcher	1888–89, 1891–92
Dave Gumpert	Pitcher	1985–86
Larry Gura	Pitcher	1970–73, 1985
Frankie Gustine	Second Base	1949
Charlie Guth	Pitcher	1880
Mark Guthrie*	Pitcher	1999–2000, 2003
Ricky Gutierrez*	Third Base	2000–01
Angel Guzman*	Pitcher	2004–05
Jose Guzman	Pitcher	1993–94

H

Eddie Haas	Outfielder	1957
Stan Hack	Third Base	1932–47
Warren Hacker	Pitcher	1948–56
Casey Hageman	Pitcher	1914
Rip Hagerman	Pitcher	1909
Luke Hagerty*	Pitcher	2005

Jerry Hairston*	Second Base	2005
Johnny Hairston	Catcher	1969
Drew Hall	Pitcher	1986–88
Jimmie Hall	Outfielder	1969–70
Mel Hall	Outfielder	1981–84
Jimmy Hallinan	Shortstop	1877–78
Steve Hamilton	Pitcher	1972
Ralph Hamner	Pitcher	1947–49
Bill Hands	Pitcher	1966–72
Chris Haney	Pitcher	1998
Fred Haney	Third Base	1927
Todd Haney	Second Base	1994–96
Frank Hankinson	Third Base	1878–79
Bill Hanlon	First Base	1903
Dave Hansen*	Third Base	1997
Ollie Hanson	Pitcher	1921
Ed Hanyzewski	Pitcher	1942–46
Bill Harbidge	Outfielder	1878–79
Lou Hardie	Catcher	1886
Bud Hardin	Shortstop	1952
Jason Hardtke	Second Base	1998
Alex Hardy	Pitcher	1902–03
Jack Hardy	Catcher	1907
Alan Hargesheimer	Pitcher	1983
Bubbles Hargrave	Catcher	1913–15
Mike Harkey	Pitcher	1988, 1990–93
Dick Harley	Outfielder	1903
Jack Harper	Pitcher	1906
Ray Harrell	Pitcher	1939
Brendan Harris*	Second Base	2004
Lenny Harris*	Third Base	2003
Vic Harris	Second Base	1974–75
Chuck Hartenstein	Pitcher	1965–68
Gabby Hartnett	Catcher	1922–40
Topsy Hartsel	Outfielder	1901
Jeff Hartsock	Pitcher	1992
Zaza Harvey	Outfielder	1900
Ron Hassey	Catcher	1984
Scott Hastings	Catcher	1875
Billy Hatcher	Outfielder	1984–85
Chris Hatcher*	Outfielder	1999–2000

Joe Hatten	Pitcher	1951–52
Grady Hatton	Third Base	1960
LaTroy Hawkins*	Pitcher	2004–05
Jack Hayden	Outfielder	1908
Bill Hayes	Catcher	1980–81
John Healy	Pitcher	1889
Bill Heath	Catcher	1969
Cliff Heathcote	Outfielder	1922–30
Mike Heathcott	Pitcher	1999–2000
Richie Hebner	Third Base	1984–85
Mike Hechinger	Catcher	1912–13
Jim Hegan	Catcher	1960
Al Heist	Outfielder	1960–61
Rollie Hemsley	Catcher	1931–32
Ken Henderson	Outfielder	1979–80
Steve Henderson	Outfielder	1981–82
Bob Hendley	Pitcher	1965–67
Harvey Hendrick	First Base	1933
Ellie Hendricks	Catcher	1972
Jack Hendricks	Outfielder	1902
Claude Hendrix	Pitcher	1916–20
George Hennessey	Pitcher	1945
Bill Henry	Pitcher	1958–59
Roy Henshaw	Pitcher	1933, 1935–36
Felix Heredia*	Pitcher	1998–2001
Babe Herman	Outfielder	1933–34
Billy Herman	Second Base	1931–41
Chad Hermansen*	Designated Hitter	2002
Gene Hermanski	Outfielder	1951–53
Chico Hernandez	Catcher	1942–43
Jose Hernandez*	Shortstop	1994–99, 2003
Ramon Hernandez	Pitcher	1968, 1976–77
Willie Hernandez	Pitcher	1977–83
Tom Hernon	Outfielder	1897
Leroy Herrmann	Pitcher	1932–33
John Herrnstein	Outfielder	1966
Buck Herzog	Second Base	1919–20
Jack Hiatt	Catcher	1970
Greg Hibbard	Pitcher	1993
John Hibbard	Pitcher	1884
Bryan Hickerson	Pitcher	1995

Eddie Hickey	Third Base	1901
Jim Hickman	Outfielder	1968–73
Kirby Higbe	Pitcher	1937–39
Irv Higginbotham	Pitcher	1909
Dick Higham	Outfielder	1875
R. E. Hildebrand	Outfielder	1902
Bobby Hill*	Second Base	2002–03
Glenallen Hill	Outfielder	1993–94, 1998–2000
Rich Hill*	Pitcher	2005
Frank Hiller	Pitcher	1950–51
Dave Hillman	Pitcher	1955–59
Paul Hines	Outfielder	1874–77
Gene Hiser	Outfielder	1971–75
Don Hoak	Third Base	1956
Glen Hobbie	Pitcher	1957–64
Billy Hoeft	Pitcher	1965–66
Guy Hoffman	Pitcher	1986
Larry Hoffman	Third Base	1901
Solly Hofman	Outfielder	1904–12, 1916
Brad Hogg	Pitcher	1915
Todd Hollandsworth*	Outfielder	2004–05
Ed Holley	Pitcher	1928
Bug Holliday	Outfielder	1885
Jessie Hollins	Pitcher	1992
John Hollison	Pitcher	1892
Charlie Hollocher	Shortstop	1918–24
Billy Holm	Catcher	1943–44
Fred Holmes	Catcher	1904
Ken Holtzman	Pitcher	1965–71, 1978–79
Marty Honan	Catcher	1890–91
Burt Hooton	Pitcher	1971–75
Trader Horne	Pitcher	1929
Rogers Hornsby	Second Base	1929–32
Tim Hosley	Catcher	1975–76
John Houseman	Second Base	1894
Tyler Houston*	Third Base	1996–99
Del Howard	Outfielder	1907–09
Cal Howe	Pitcher	1952
Jay Howell	Pitcher	1981

Mike Hubbard	Catcher	1995–97
Trenidad Hubbard*	Outfielder	2003
Ken Hubbs	Second Base	1961–63
Johnny Hudson	Second Base	1941
Jim Hughes	Pitcher	1956
Joe Hughes	Outfielder	1902
Roy Hughes	Second Base	1944–45
Terry Hughes	Third Base	1970
Tom Hughes	Pitcher	1900–01
Jim Hughey	Pitcher	1893
Bob Humphreys	Pitcher	1965
Bert Humphries	Pitcher	1913–15
Randy Hundley	Catcher	1966–73, 1976–77
Todd Hundley	Catcher	2001–02
Herb Hunter	Third Base	1916–17
Walt Huntzinger	Pitcher	1926
Don Hurst	First Base	1934
Jeff Huson	Shortstop	2000
Ed Hutchinson	Second Base	1890
Bill Hutchison	Pitcher	1889–95
Herb Hutson	Pitcher	1974

I

Blaise Ilsley	Pitcher	1994
Monte Irvin	Outfielder	1956
Charlie Irwin	Third Base	1893–95
Frank Isbell	First Base	1898

J

Damian Jackson*	Second Base	2004
Danny Jackson	Pitcher	1991–92
Darrin Jackson	Outfielder	1985, 1987–89
Larry Jackson	Pitcher	1963–66
Randy Jackson	Third Base	1950–55, 1959
Lou Jackson	Outfielder	1958–59
Nic Jackson*	Left Field	2004
Elmer Jacobs	Pitcher	1924–25
Mike Jacobs	Shortstop	1902
Ray Jacobs	—	1928

Tony Jacobs	Pitcher	1948
Merwin Jacobson	Outfielder	1916
Jake Jaeckel	Pitcher	1964
Joe Jaeger	Pitcher	1920
Art Jahn	Outfielder	1925
Cleo James	Outfielder	1970–71, 1973
Rick James	Pitcher	1967
Hal Jeffcoat	Outfielder	1948–55
Frank Jelincich	Outfielder	1941
Fergie Jenkins	Pitcher	1966–1973, 1982–83
Doug Jennings	Outfielder	1993
Robin Jennings	Outfielder	1996–97, 1999
Garry Jestadt	Third Base	1971
Manny Jimenez	Outfielder	1969
Abe Johnson	Pitcher	1893
Ben Johnson	Pitcher	1959–60
Bill Johnson	Pitcher	1983–84
Cliff Johnson	Designated Hitter	1980
Davey Johnson	Second Base	1978
Don Johnson	Second Base	1943–48
Footer Johnson	—	1958
Howard Johnson	Third Base	1995
Ken Johnson	Pitcher	1969
Lance Johnson	Outfielder	1997–99
Lou Johnson	Outfielder	1960, 1968
Mark Johnson*	Catcher	2005
Jay Johnstone	Outfielder	1982–84
Jimmy Johnston	Third Base	1914
Roy Joiner	Pitcher	1934–35
Charley Jones	Outfielder	1877
Clarence Jones	Outfielder	1967–68
Davy Jones	Outfielder	1902–04
Doug Jones	Pitcher	1996
Percy Jones	Pitcher	1920–22, 1925–28
Sam Jones	Pitcher	1955–56
Sheldon Jones	Pitcher	1953
Claude Jonnard	Pitcher	1929
Billy Jurges	Shortstop	1931–38, 1946–47

K

Mike Kahoe	Catcher	1901–02, 1907
Don Kaiser	Pitcher	1955–57
Al Kaiser	Outfielder	1911
John Kane	Outfielder	1909–10
Matt Karchner	Pitcher	1998–2000
Eric Karros	First Base	2003
Jack Katoll	Pitcher	1898–99
Tony Kaufmann	Pitcher	1921–27
Teddy Kearns	First Base	1924–25
Chick Keating	Shortstop	1913–15
Vic Keen	Pitcher	1921–25
George Keerl	Second Base	1875
John Kelleher	Third Base	1921–23
Mick Kelleher	Shortstop	1976–80
Frank Kellert	First Base	1956
Bob Kelly	Pitcher	1951–53
George Kelly	First Base	1930
King Kelly	Outfielder	1880–86
Joe Kelly	Outfielder	1916
Joe Kelly	Outfielder	1926, 1928
David Kelton*	Outfielder	2003–04
Junior Kennedy	Second Base	1982–83
Snapper Kennedy	Outfielder	1902
Ted Kennedy	Pitcher	1885
Marty Keough	Outfielder	1966
Matt Keough	Pitcher	1986
Mel Kerr	—	1925
Don Kessinger	Shortstop	1964–75
Brooks Kieschnick*	Pitcher	1996–97
Pete Kilduff	Second Base	1917–19
Paul Kilgus	Pitcher	1989
Bill Killefer	Catcher	1918–21
Frank Killen	Pitcher	1900
Matt Kilroy	Pitcher	1898
Newt Kimball	Pitcher	1937–38
Bruce Kimm	Catcher	1979
Jerry Kindall	Second Base	1956–58, 1960–61
Ralph Kiner	Outfielder	1953–54

Chick King	Outfielder	1958–59
Jim King	Outfielder	1955–56
Ray King*	Pitcher	1999
Dave Kingman	Outfielder	1978–80
Walt Kinzie	Shortstop	1884
Jim Kirby	—	1949
Chris Kitsos	Shortstop	1954
Malachi Kittridge	Catcher	1890–97
Chuck Klein	Outfielder	1934–36
Johnny Kling	Catcher	1900–08, 1910–11
Johnny Klippstein	Pitcher	1950–54
Joe Klugmann	Second Base	1921–22
Joe Kmak	Catcher	1995
Otto Knabe	Second Base	1916
Pete Knisely	Outfielder	1913–15
Darold Knowles	Pitcher	1975–76
Mark Koenig	Shortstop	1932–33
Elmer Koestner	Pitcher	1914
Cal Koonce	Pitcher	1962–67
Casey Kopitzke*	Catcher	2005
John Koronka*	Pitcher	2005
Jim Korwan	Pitcher	1897
Fabian Kowalik	Pitcher	1935–36
Joe Kraemer	Pitcher	1989–90
Randy Kramer	Pitcher	1990
Ken Kravec	Pitcher	1981–82
Mike Kreevich	Outfielder	1931
Mickey Kreitner	Catcher	1943–44
Jim Kremmel	Pitcher	1974
Bill Krieg	Catcher	1885
Gus Krock	Pitcher	1888–89
Rube Kroh	Pitcher	1908–10
Chris Krug	Catcher	1965–66
Gene Krug	—	1981
Marty Krug	Third Base	1922
Mike Krukow	Pitcher	1976–81
Harvey Kuenn	Outfielder	1965–66
Jeff Kunkel	Shortstop	1992
Emil Kush	Pitcher	1941–42, 1946–49

L

Tony La Russa	Second Base	1973
Dave LaRoche	Pitcher	1973–74
Pete Lacock	First Base	1972–76
Kerry Lacy	Pitcher	2000
Doyle Lade	Pitcher	1946–50
Steve Lake	Catcher	1983–86, 1993
Jack Lamabe	Pitcher	1968
Pete Lamers	Catcher	1902
Dennis Lamp	Pitcher	1977–80
Les Lancaster	Pitcher	1987–91
Hobie Landrith	Catcher	1956
Bill Landrum	Pitcher	1988
Ced Landrum	Outfielder	1991
Don Landrum	Outfielder	1962–65
Walt Lanfranconi	Pitcher	1941
Bill Lange	Outfielder	1893–99
Terry Larkin	Pitcher	1878–79
Vic Larose	Second Base	1968
Dan Larson	Pitcher	1982
Don Larsen	Pitcher	1967
Al Lary	Pitcher	1954–55, 1962
Chuck Lauer	Outfielder	1890
Jimmy Lavender	Pitcher	1912–16
Vance Law	Third Base	1988–89
Matt Lawton*	Outfielder	2005
Tony Lazzeri	Second Base	1938
Tommy Leach	Outfielder	1912–14
Fred Lear	Third Base	1918–19
Hal Leathers	Shortstop	1920
Bill Lee	Pitcher	1934–43, 1947
Don Lee	Pitcher	1966
Derrek Lee*	First Base	2004–05
Tom Lee	Pitcher	1884
Craig Lefferts	Pitcher	1983
Hank Leiber	Outfielder	1939–41
Jon Leicester*	Pitcher	2004–05
Lefty Leifield	Pitcher	1912–13
Dick Lemay	Pitcher	1963
Dave Lemonds	Pitcher	1969
Bob Lennon	Outfielder	1957
Ed Lennox	Third Base	1912
Dutch Leonard	Pitcher	1949–53
Roy Leslie	First Base	1917
Darren Lewis	Outfielder	2002
Richard Lewis*	Second Base	2004–05
Carlos Lezcano	Outfielder	1980–81
Jon Lieber*	Pitcher	1999–2002
Gene Lillard	Pitcher	1936, 1939
Freddie Lindstrom	Third Base	1935
Cole Liniak	Third Base	1999–2000
Dick Littlefield	Pitcher	1957
Jack Littrell	Shortstop	1957
Mickey Livingston	Catcher	1943, 1945–47
Hans Lobert	Third Base	1905
Bob Locker	Pitcher	1973, 1975
Kenny Lofton*	Outfielder	2003
Bob Logan	Pitcher	1937–38
Bill Long	Pitcher	1990
Dale Long	First Base	1957–59
Davey Lopes	Second Base	1984–86
Andrew Lorraine*	Pitcher	1999–2000
Jay Loviglio	Second Base	1983
Grover Lowdermilk	Pitcher	1912
Bobby Lowe	Second Base	1902–03
Terrell Lowery	Outfielder	1997–98
Turk Lown	Pitcher	1951–54, 1956–58
Peanuts Lowrey	Outfielder	1942–43, 1945–49
Pat Luby	Pitcher	1890–92
Fred Luderus	First Base	1909–10
Mike Lum	Outfielder	1981
Fernando Lunar*	Catcher	2004
Carl Lundgren	Pitcher	1902–09
Tom Lundstedt	Catcher	1973–74
Keith Luuloa*	Shortstop	2000
Ed Lynch	Pitcher	1986–87
Danny Lynch	Second Base	1948
Henry Lynch	Outfielder	1893
Mike Lynch	Outfielder	1902
Tom Lynch	Pitcher	1884

Red Lynn	Pitcher	1944		Doc Marshall	Catcher	1908
Dad Lytle	Second Base	1890		Jim Marshall	First Base	1958–59
				Frank Martin	Third Base	1898
M				J. C. Martin	Catcher	1970–72
Robert Machado*	Catcher	2001–02		Jerry Martin	Outfielder	1979–80
Jose Macias*	Third Base	2004–05		Mike Martin	Catcher	1986
Bill Mack	Pitcher	1908		Morrie Martin	Pitcher	1959
Ray Mack	Second Base	1947		Speed Martin	Pitcher	1918–22
Steve Macko	Second Base	1979–80		Stu Martin	Second Base	1943
Len Madden	Pitcher	1912		Carmelo Martinez	Outfielder	1983
Clarence Maddern	Outfielder	1946, 1948–49		Dave Martinez	Outfielder	1986–88, 2000
Greg Maddux*	Pitcher	1986–92,		Felix Martinez*	Second Base	2004
		2004–05		Ramon Martinez*	Shortstop	2003–04
Bill Madlock	Third Base	1974–76		Sandy Martinez*	Catcher	1998–99
Sal Madrid	Shortstop	1947		Joe Marty	Outfielder	1937–39
Dave Magadan	Third Base	1996		Randy Martz	Pitcher	1980–82
Lee Magee	Outfielder	1919		Mike Mason	Pitcher	1987
George Magoon	Shortstop	1899		Gordon Massa	Catcher	1957–58
Freddie Maguire	Second Base	1928		Nelson Mathews	Outfielder	1960–63
Ron Mahay*	Pitcher	2001–02		Gary Matthews*	Center Field	2000–01
Pat Mahomes*	Pitcher	2002		Gary Matthews	Outfielder	1984–87
Mike Mahoney*	Catcher	2000, 2002		Bobby Mattick	Shortstop	1938–40
Willard Mains	Pitcher	1888		Gene Mauch	Second Base	1948–49
Oswaldo Mairena*	Pitcher	2000		Hal Mauck	Pitcher	1893
George Maisel	Outfielder	1921–22		Carmen Mauro	Outfielder	1948, 1950–51
Mike Maksudian	First Base	1994		Jason Maxwell*	Second Base	1998
John Malarkey	Pitcher	1899		Derrick May	Outfielder	1990–94
Candy Maldonado	Outfielder	1993		Jakie May	Pitcher	1931–32
Fergy Malone	Catcher	1874		Scott May	Pitcher	1991
Pat Malone	Pitcher	1928–34		Ed Mayer	Pitcher	1957–58
Billy Maloney	Outfielder	1905		Bill McAfee	Pitcher	1930
Gus Mancuso	Catcher	1939		Jim McAnany	Outfielder	1961–62
Hal Manders	Pitcher	1946		Ike McAuley	Shortstop	1925
Les Mann	Outfielder	1916–19		Algie McBride	Outfielder	1896
Garth Mann	—	1944		Bill McCabe	Outfielder	1918–20
David Manning*	Pitcher	2004		Dutch McCall	Pitcher	1948
Dick Manville	Pitcher	1952		Alex McCarthy	Second Base	1915–16
Rabbit Maranville	Shortstop	1925		Jack McCarthy	Outfielder	1900, 1903–05
Gonzalo Marquez	First Base	1973–74		Jim McCauley	Catcher	1885
Luis Marquez	Outfielder	1954		Harry McChesney	Outfielder	1904
William Marriott	Third Base	1917, 1920–21		Scott McClain*	First Base	2005

Bill McClellan	Second Base	1878	Lennie Merullo	Shortstop	1941–47
Lloyd McClendon	Outfielder	1989–90	Steve Mesner	Third Base	1938–39
George McConnell	Pitcher	1914, 1916	Catfish Metkovich	Outfielder	1953
Jim McCormick	Pitcher	1885–86	Roger Metzger	Shortstop	1970
Barry McCormick	Third Base	1896–1901	Alex Metzler	Outfielder	1925
Clyde McCullough	Catcher	1940–43,	Dutch Meyer	Second Base	1937
		1946–48, 1953–56	Russ Meyer	Pitcher	1946–48, 1956
Lindy McDaniel	Pitcher	1963–65	Levi Meyerle	Third Base	1874
Ed McDonald	Third Base	1913	Chad Meyers*	Second Base	1999–2001
Chuck McElroy*	Pitcher	1991–93	Ralph Michaels	Third Base	1924–26
Monte McFarland	Pitcher	1895–96	Ed Mickelson	First Base	1957
Willie McGill	Pitcher	1893–94	Matt Mieske	Outfielder	1998
Dan McGinn	Pitcher	1972	Pete Mikkelsen	Pitcher	1967–68
Gus McGinnis	Pitcher	1893	Hank Miklos	Pitcher	1944
Kevin McGlinchy*	Pitcher	2004	Eddie Miksis	Second Base	1951–56
Lynn McGlothen	Pitcher	1978–81	Bob Miller	Pitcher	1970–71
Fred McGriff*	First Base	2001–02	Damian Miller*	Catcher	2003
Harry McIntire	Pitcher	1910–12	Doc Miller	Outfielder	1910
Jim McKnight	Third Base	1960, 1962	Dusty Miller	Outfielder	1902
Polly McLarry	Second Base	1915	Hack Miller	Outfielder	1922–25
Larry McLean	Catcher	1903	Joe Miller	Second Base	1875
Cal McLish	Pitcher	1949, 1951	Kurt Miller	Pitcher	1998–99
Jimmy McMath	Outfielder	1968	Ox Miller	Pitcher	1947
Greg McMichael	Pitcher	2000	Ward Miller	Outfielder	1912–13
Norm McMillan	Third Base	1928–29	George Milstead	Pitcher	1924–26
Brian McNichol*	Pitcher	1999	Paul Minner	Pitcher	1950–56
Brian McRae	Outfielder	1995–97	Mike Mitchell	Outfielder	1913
Cal McVey	First Base	1876–77	Sergio Mitre*	Pitcher	2003–05
George Meakim	Pitcher	1892	George Mitterwald	Catcher	1974–77
Russ Meers	Pitcher	1941, 1946–47	Bill Moisan	Pitcher	1953
Dave Meier	Outfielder	1988	Jose Molina*	Catcher	1999
Sam Mejias	Outfielder	1979	Bob Molinaro	Outfielder	1982
Jock Menefee	Pitcher	1900–03	Fritz Mollwitz	First Base	1913–14, 1916
Rudy Meoli	Shortstop	1978	Rick Monday	Outfielder	1972–76
Orlando Merced*	Outfielder	1998	Al Montreuil	Second Base	1972
Kent Mercker*	Pitcher	2004	George Moolic	Catcher	1886
Ron Meridith	Pitcher	1984–85	Charley Moore	Shortstop	1912
Fred Merkle	First Base	1917–20	Donnie Moore	Pitcher	1975, 1977–79
Lloyd Merriman	Outfielder	1955	Earl Moore	Pitcher	1913
Bill Merritt	Catcher	1891	Johnny Moore	Outfielder	1928–29,
Sam Mertes	Outfielder	1898–1900			1931, 1932, 1945

Jake Mooty	Pitcher	1940–43
Jerry Morales	Outfielder	1974–77,
		1981–83
Bill Moran	Catcher	1895
Pat Moran	Catcher	1906–09
Mickey Morandini	Second Base	1998–99
Seth Morehead	Pitcher	1959–60
Ramon Morel	Pitcher	1997
Keith Moreland	Outfielder	1982–87
Bobby Morgan	Second Base	1957–58
Mike Morgan	Pitcher	1992–95,
		1998
Vern Morgan	Third Base	1954–55
Moe Morhardt	First Base	1961–62
George Moriarty	Third Base	1903–04
Jim Moroney	Pitcher	1912
Ed Morris	Pitcher	1922
Frank Morrissey	Pitcher	1902
Walt Moryn	Outfielder	1956–60
Paul Moskau	Pitcher	1983
Jim Mosolf	Outfielder	1933
Mal Moss	Pitcher	1930
Jamie Moyer*	Pitcher	1986–88
Phil Mudrock	Pitcher	1963
Bill Mueller*	Third Base	2001–02
Terry Mulholland*	Pitcher	1997–99
Eddie Mulligan	Third Base	1915–16
Jerry Mumphrey	Outfielder	1986–88
Bob Muncrief	Pitcher	1949
Joe Munson	Outfielder	1925–26
Bobby Murcer	Outfielder	1977–79
Danny Murphy	Pitcher	1960–62
Calvin Murray*	Outfielder	2004
Jim Murray	Outfielder	1902
Red Murray	Outfielder	1915
Tony Murray	Outfielder	1923
Matt Murton*	Left Field	2005
Billy Myers	Shortstop	1941
Randy Myers	Pitcher	1993–95
Richie Myers	—	1956
Rodney Myers*	Pitcher	1996–99

N

Chris Nabholz	Pitcher	1995
Tom Nagle	Catcher	1890–91
Buddy Napier	Pitcher	1918
Joey Nation*	Pitcher	2000
Jaime Navarro	Pitcher	1995–96
Tom Needham	Catcher	1909–14
Cal Neeman	Catcher	1957–60
Art Nehf	Pitcher	1927–29
Lynn Nelson	Pitcher	1930,
		1933–34
Dick Nen	First Base	1968
Joel Newkirk	Pitcher	1919–20
Charlie Newman	Outfielder	1892
Ray Newman	Pitcher	1971
Bobo Newsom	Pitcher	1932
Art Nichols	Catcher	1898–1900
Dolan Nichols	Pitcher	1958
Bill Nicholson	Outfielder	1939–48
George Nicol	Outfielder	1891
Hugh Nicol	Outfielder	1881–82
Joe Niekro	Pitcher	1967–69
Jose Nieves*	Shortstop	1998–2000
Al Nipper	Pitcher	1988
Paul Noce	Second Base	1987
Dickie Noles	Pitcher	1982–84, 1987
Hideo Nomo*	Pitcher	1999
Pete Noonan	Catcher	1906
Wayne Nordhagen	Outfielder	1983
Irv Noren	Outfielder	1959–60
Fred Norman	Pitcher	1964,
		1966–67
Billy North	Outfielder	1971–72
Ron Northey	Outfielder	1950, 1952
Phil Norton*	Pitcher	2000, 2003
Don Nottebart	Pitcher	1969
Lou Novikoff	Outfielder	1941–44
Roberto Novoa*	Pitcher	2005
Rube Novotney	Catcher	1949
Jose Antonio Nunez*	Pitcher	1990
Rich Nye	Pitcher	1966–69

O

Mike O'Berry	Catcher	1980
John O'Brien	Second Base	1893
Pete O'Brien	Second Base	1890
Johnny O'Connor	Catcher	1916
Ken O'Dea	Catcher	1935–38
Bob O'Farrell	Catcher	1915–25, 1934
Hal O'Hagen	First Base	1902
Troy O'Leary*	Outfielder	2003
Emmett O'Neill	Pitcher	1946
Jack O'Neill	Catcher	1904–05
Will Ohman*	Pitcher	2000–01, 2005
Augie Ojeda*	Shortstop	2000–03
Gene Oliver	Catcher	1968–69
Nate Oliver	Second Base	1969
Barney Olsen	Outfielder	1941
Vern Olsen	Pitcher	1939–42, 1946
Steve Ontiveros	Third Base	1977–80
Rey Ordonez*	Shortstop	2004
Kevin Orie*	First Base	1997–98, 2002
Jose Ortiz	Outfielder	1971
Bob Osborn	Pitcher	1925–27, 1929–30
Donovan Osborne*	Pitcher	2002
Tiny Osborne	Pitcher	1922–24
Johnny Ostrowski	Outfielder	1943–46
Reggie Otero	First Base	1945
Billy Ott	Outfielder	1962, 1964
Dave Otto	Pitcher	1994
Orval Overall	Pitcher	1906–10, 1913
Ernie Ovitz	Pitcher	1911
Dave Owen	Shortstop	1983–85
Mickey Owen	Catcher	1949–51

P

Gene Packard	Pitcher	1916–17
Andy Pafko	Outfielder	1943–51
Vance Page	Pitcher	1938–41
Karl Pagel	First Base	1978–79
Donn Pall	Pitcher	1994
Rafael Palmeiro*	First Base	1986–88

Erik Pappas	Catcher	1991
Milt Pappas	Pitcher	1970–73
Mark Parent	Catcher	1994–95
Doc Parker	Pitcher	1893, 1895–96
Roy Parmelee	Pitcher	1937
Jiggs Parrott	Third Base	1892–95
Tom Parrott	Outfielder	1893
Dode Paskert	Outfielder	1918–20
Claude Passeau	Pitcher	1939–47
Bob Patterson	Pitcher	1996–98
Corey Patterson*	Center Field	2000–05
Ken Patterson	Pitcher	1992
Reggie Patterson	Pitcher	1983–85
Josh Paul*	Catcher	2003
Mike Paul	Pitcher	1973–74
Dave Pavlas	Pitcher	1990–91
Ted Pawelek	Catcher	1946
George Pearce	Pitcher	1912–16
Charlie Pechous	Third Base	1916–17
Jorge Pedre	Catcher	1992
Chick Pedroes	Outfielder	1902
Roberto Pena	Shortstop	1965–66
Ken Penner	Pitcher	1929
Joe Pepitone	First Base	1970–73
Mike Perez	Pitcher	1995–96
Neifi Perez*	Shortstop	2004–05
Yorkis Perez*	Pitcher	1991
Harry Perkowski	Pitcher	1955
Jon Perlman	Pitcher	1985
Pat Perry	Pitcher	1988–89
Scott Perry	Pitcher	1916
John Peters	Shortstop	1874–77, 1879
Bob Pettit	Outfielder	1887–88
Jesse Petty	Pitcher	1930
Fred Pfeffer	Second Base	1883–89, 1891, 1896–97
Jeff Pfeffer	Pitcher	1905, 1910
Jack Pfiester	Pitcher	1906–11
Art Phelan	Third Base	1913–15
Babe Phelps	Catcher	1933–34
Adolfo Phillips	Outfielder	1966–69

Taylor Phillips	Pitcher	1958–59		**Q**		
Tom Phoebus	Pitcher	1972		Jim Qualls	Outfielder	1969
Bill Phyle	Pitcher	1898–99		Joe Quest	Second Base	1879–82
Charlie Pick	Second Base	1918–19		Ruben Quevedo*	Pitcher	2000
Eddie Pick	Third Base	1927		Frank Quinn	Outfielder	1899
Jeff Pico	Pitcher	1988–90		Joe Quinn	Catcher	1877
Ray Pierce	Pitcher	1924		Paddy Quinn	Catcher	1875
Andy Piercy	Second Base	1881		Wimpy Quinn	Pitcher	1941
Bill Piercy	Pitcher	1926		Luis Quinones	Third Base	1987
George Piktuzis	Pitcher	1956				
Horacio Pina	Pitcher	1974		**R**		
Renyel Pinto*	Pitcher	2004–05		Dick Radatz	Pitcher	1967
Marc Pisciotta	Pitcher	1997–98		Dave Rader	Catcher	1978
Pinky Pittinger	Shortstop	1925		Ken Raffensberger	Pitcher	1940–41
Juan Pizarro	Pitcher	1970–73		Pat Ragan	Pitcher	1909
Whitey Platt	Outfielder	1942–43		Steve Rain*	Pitcher	1999–2000
Dan Plesac	Pitcher	1993–94		Chuck Rainey	Pitcher	1983–84
Bill Plummer	Catcher	1968		Bob Ramazzotti	Second Base	1949–53
Tom Poholsky	Pitcher	1957		Aramis Ramirez*	Third Base	2003–05
Howie Pollet	Pitcher	1953–55		Domingo Ramos	Shortstop	1989–90
Elmer Ponder	Pitcher	1921		Willie Ramsdell	Pitcher	1952
Tom Poorman	Outfielder	1880		Fernando Ramsey	Outfielder	1992
Paul Popovich	Second Base	1964, 1966, 1969–73		Newt Randall	Outfielder	1907
				Len Randle	Third Base	1980
Bo Porter*	Outfielder	1999		Jaisen Randolph*	—	2001
Bob Porterfield	Pitcher	1959		Merritt Ranew	Catcher	1963–64
Bill Powell	Pitcher	1912		Cody Ransom*	Shortstop	2005
Phil Powers	Catcher	1878		Dennis Rasmussen	Pitcher	1992
Willie Prall	Pitcher	1975		Tommy Raub	Catcher	1903
Johnny Pramesa	Catcher	1952		Bob Raudman	Outfielder	1966–67
Andy Pratt*	Pitcher	2004		Fred Raymer	Second Base	1901
Todd Pratt*	Catcher	1995		Frank Reberger	Pitcher	1968
Mike Prendergast	Pitcher	1916–17		Jeff Reed	Catcher	1999–2000
Tot Pressnell	Pitcher	1941–42		Phil Regan	Pitcher	1968–72
Ray Prim	Pitcher	1943, 1945–46		Herman Reich	First Base	1949
Don Prince	Pitcher	1962		Hal Reilly	Outfielder	1919
Mark Prior*	Pitcher	2002–05		Josh Reilly	Second Base	1896
Mike Proly	Pitcher	1982–83		Laurie Reis	Pitcher	1877–78
Ed Putman	Catcher	1976, 1978		Ken Reitz	Third Base	1981
John Pyecha	Pitcher	1954		Mike Remlinger*	Pitcher	2003–05
Shadow Pyle	Pitcher	1887		Jack Remsen	Outfielder	1878–79

Name	Position	Years
Laddie Renfroe	Pitcher	1991
Steve Renko	Pitcher	1976–77
Ed Reulbach	Pitcher	1905–13
Paul Reuschel	Pitcher	1975–78
Rick Reuschel	Pitcher	1972–81, 1983–84
Archie Reynolds	Pitcher	1968–70
Carl Reynolds	Outfielder	1937–39
Bob Rhoads	Pitcher	1902
Karl Rhodes	Outfielder	1993–95
Del Rice	Catcher	1960
Hal Rice	Outfielder	1954
Len Rice	Catcher	1945
Fred Richards	First Base	1951
Lance Richbourg	Outfielder	1932
Lew Richie	Pitcher	1910–13
Beryl Richmond	Pitcher	1933
Reggie Richter	Pitcher	1911
Marv Rickert	Outfielder	1942, 1946–47
George Riley	Pitcher	1979–80
Allen Ripley	Pitcher	1982
Roberto Rivera	Pitcher	1995
Mel Roach	Second Base	1961
Skel Roach	Pitcher	1899
Fred Roat	Third Base	1892
Kevin Roberson	Outfielder	1993–95
Dave Roberts	Pitcher	1977–78
Robin Roberts	Pitcher	1966
Daryl Robertson	Shortstop	1962
Dave Robertson	Outfielder	1919–21
Don Robertson	Outfielder	1954
Jeff Robinson	Pitcher	1992
Andre Rodgers	Shortstop	1961–64
Freddy Rodriguez	Pitcher	1958
Henry Rodriguez*	Left Field	1998–00
Roberto Rodriquez	Pitcher	1970
Billy Rogell	Shortstop	1940
Russ Rohlicek*	Pitcher	2004–05
Dan Rohn	Second Base	1983–84
Mel Rojas	Pitcher	1997
Rolando Roomes	Outfielder	1988
Charlie Root	Pitcher	1926–41
Dave Rosello	Second Base	1972–77
John Roskos*	Outfielder	2001
Gary Ross	Pitcher	1968–69
Jack Rowan	Pitcher	1911
Wade Rowdon	Third Base	1987
Dave Rowe	Outfielder	1877
Luther Roy	Pitcher	1927
Vic Roznovsky	Catcher	1964–65
Dutch Rudolph	Outfielder	1904
Ken Rudolph	Catcher	1969–73
Dutch Ruether	Pitcher	1917
Glendon Rusch*	Pitcher	2004–05
Bob Rush	Pitcher	1948–57
Jack Russell	Pitcher	1938–39
Rip Russell	First Base	1939–42
Dick Ruthven	Pitcher	1983–86
Jason Ryan*	Pitcher	1999
Jimmy Ryan	Outfielder	1885–89, 1891–1900

S

Name	Position	Years
Vic Saier	First Base	1911–17
Luis Salazar	Third Base	1989–92
Angel Salazar	Shortstop	1988
Felix Sanchez*	Pitcher	2003
Jesus Sanchez*	Pitcher	2002
Rey Sanchez*	Shortstop	1991–97
Ryne Sandberg	Second Base	1982–94, 1996–97
Scott Sanders*	Pitcher	1999
Scott Sanderson	Pitcher	1984–89
Benito Santiago*	Catcher	1999
Ron Santo	Third Base	1960–73
Ed Sauer	Outfielder	1943–45
Hank Sauer	Outfielder	1949–55
Ted Savage	Outfielder	1967–68
Carl Sawatski	Catcher	1948, 1950, 1953
Bob Scanlan	Pitcher	1991–93
Germany Schaefer	Second Base	1901–02
Jimmie Schaffer	Catcher	1963–64
Joe Schaffernoth	Pitcher	1959–61

Bob Scheffing	Catcher	1941–42, 1946–50
Hank Schenz	Second Base	1946–49
Morrie Schick	Outfielder	1917
Calvin Schiraldi	Pitcher	1988–89
Larry Schlafly	Second Base	1902
Freddy Schmidt	Pitcher	1947
Johnny Schmitz	Pitcher	1941–42, 1946–51
Ed Schorr	Pitcher	1915
Paul Schramka	Outfielder	1953
Hank Schreiber	Third Base	1926
Pop Schriver	Catcher	1891–94
Al Schroll	Pitcher	1960
Art Schult	First Base	1959–60
Frank Schulte	Outfielder	1904–16
Johnny Schulte	Catcher	1929
Barney Schultz	Pitcher	1961–63
Bob Schultz	Pitcher	1951–53
Buddy Schultz	Pitcher	1975–76
Don Schulze	Pitcher	1983–84
Joe Schultz	Outfielder	1915
Wayne Schurr	Pitcher	1964
Bill Schuster	Shortstop	1943–45
Rudy Schwenck	Pitcher	1909
Dick Scott	Pitcher	1964
Gary Scott	Third Base	1991–92
Milt Scott	First Base	1882
Pete Scott	Outfielder	1926–27
Rodney Scott	Second Base	1978
Tom Seaton	Pitcher	1916–17
Frank Secory	Outfielder	1944–46
Herman Segelke	Pitcher	1982
Kurt Seibert	Second Base	1979
Bill Selby*	Third Base	2003–04
Dick Selma	Pitcher	1969
Mike Sember	Third Base	1977–78
Manny Seoane	Pitcher	1978
Dan Serafini*	Pitcher	1999
Bill Serena	Third Base	1949–54
Scott Servais	Catcher	1995–98

Tommy Sewell	—	1927
Orator Shaffer	Outfielder	1879
Art Shamsky	Outfielder	1972
Red Shannon	Second Base	1926
Bobby Shantz	Pitcher	1964
Bob Shaw	Pitcher	1967
Sam Shaw	Pitcher	1893
Marty Shay	Second Base	1916
Danny Sheaffer	Catcher	1998–99
Al Shealy	Pitcher	1930
Dave Shean	Second Base	1911
Jimmy Sheckard	Outfielder	1906–12
Tommy Shields	Second Base	1993
Clyde Shoun	Pitcher	1935–37
Terry Shumpert*	Second Base	1996
Ed Sicking	Second Base	1916
Walter Signer	Pitcher	1943, 1945
Charlie Silvera	Catcher	1957
Curt Simmons	Pitcher	1966–67
Randall Simon*	First Base	2003
Duke Simpson	Pitcher	1953
Elmer Singleton	Pitcher	1957–59
Ted Sizemore	Second Base	1979
Roe Skidmore	—	1970
Jimmy Slagle	Outfielder	1902–08
Cy Slapnicka	Pitcher	1911
Sterling Slaughter	Pitcher	1964
Lefty Sloat	Pitcher	1949
Heathcliff Slocumb	Pitcher	1991–93
Roy Smalley	Shortstop	1948–53
Charlie Smith	Pitcher	1911–14
Aleck Smith	Catcher	1904
Bob Smith	Pitcher	1931–32
Bob Smith	Pitcher	1959
Bobby Gene Smith	Outfielder	1962
Bull Smith	Outfielder	1906
Charley Smith	Third Base	1969
Dave Smith	Pitcher	1991–92
Dwight Smith	Outfielder	1989–93
Earl Smith	Outfielder	1916
Greg Smith	Second Base	1989–90

Harry Smith	Second Base	1877	Randy Stein	Pitcher		1982
Jason Smith*	First Base	2001	Harry Steinfeldt	Third Base		1906–10
Lee Smith	Pitcher	1980–87	Rick Stelmaszek	Catcher		1974
Paul Smith	First Base	1958	Jake Stenzel	Outfielder		1890
Willie Smith	Outfielder	1968–70	Earl Stephenson	Pitcher		1971
Steve Smyth*	Pitcher	2002	Joe Stephenson	Catcher		1944
Marcelino Solis	Pitcher	1958	John Stephenson	Catcher		1967–68
Eddie Solomon	Pitcher	1975	Phil Stephenson	First Base		1989
Pete Sommers	Catcher	1889	Riggs Stephenson	Outfielder		1926–34
Rudy Sommers	Pitcher	1912	Walter Stephenson	Catcher		1935–36
Lary Sorensen	Pitcher	1985	Dave Stevens	Pitcher		1997–98
Sammy Sosa*	Outfielder	1992–2004	Ace Stewart	Second Base		1895
Geovany Soto*	Catcher	2005	Jimmy Stewart	Outfielder		1963–67
Al Spalding	Pitcher	1876–78	Mack Stewart	Pitcher		1944–45
Al Spangler	Outfielder	1967–71	Tuffy Stewart	Outfielder		1913–14
Bob Speake	Outfielder	1955, 1957	Tim Stoddard	Pitcher		1984
Chris Speier	Shortstop	1985–86	Steve Stone	Pitcher		1974–76
Justin Speier*	Pitcher	1998	Bill Stoneman	Pitcher		1967–68
Rob Sperring	Second Base	1974–76	Joe Strain	Second Base		1981
Carl Spongberg	Pitcher	1908	Sammy Strang	Third Base		1900, 1902
Jerry Spradlin*	Pitcher	2000	Doug Strange	Third Base		1991–92
Charlie Sprague	Outfielder	1887	Scott Stratton	Pitcher		1894–95
Jack Spring	Pitcher	1964	Lou Stringer	Second Base		1941–42, 1946
Jim St.Vrain	Pitcher	1902	George Stueland	Pitcher		1921–23, 1925
Eddie Stack	Pitcher	1913–14	Bobby Sturgeon	Shortstop		1940–42,
Scott Stahoviak	First Base	1999				1946–47
Tuck Stainback	Outfielder	1934–37	Tanyon Sturtze*	Pitcher		1995–96
Matt Stairs*	Outfielder	2001	Chris Stynes*	Third Base		2002
Gale Staley	Second Base	1925	Bill Sullivan	Outfielder		1878
Pete Standridge	Pitcher	1915	John Sullivan	Outfielder		1921
Eddie Stanky	Second Base	1943–44	Marty Sullivan	Outfielder		1887–88
Joe Stanley	Outfielder	1909	Mike Sullivan	Pitcher		1890
Tom Stanton	Catcher	1904	Champ Summers	Outfielder		1975–76
Ray Starr	Pitcher	1945	Billy Sunday	Outfielder		1883–87
Joe Start	First Base	1878	Jim Sundberg	Catcher		1987–88
Jigger Statz	Outfielder	1922–25	Rick Sutcliffe	Pitcher		1984–91
Ed Stauffer	Pitcher	1923	Sy Sutcliffe	Catcher		1884–85
John Stedronsky	Third Base	1879	Bruce Sutter	Pitcher		1976–80
Kennie Steenstra	Pitcher	1998	Dave Swartzbaugh	Pitcher		1995–97
Morrie Steevens	Pitcher	1962	Bill Sweeney	Second Base		1907, 1914
Ed Stein	Pitcher	1890–91	Les Sweetland	Pitcher		1931

Steve Swisher	Catcher	1974–77
Jason Szuminski*	Pitcher	2004
T		
Jerry Tabb	First Base	1976
Pat Tabler	First Base	1981–82
Bob Talbot	Outfielder	1953–54
Chuck Tanner	Outfielder	1957–58
Kevin Tapani	Pitcher	1997–2001
El Tappe	Catcher	1954–56, 1958, 1960, 1962
Ted Tappe	Outfielder	1955
Bennie Tate	Catcher	1934
Ramon Tatis	Pitcher	1997
Julian Tavarez*	Pitcher	2001
Chink Taylor	Outfielder	1925
Danny Taylor	Outfielder	1929–32
Harry Taylor	First Base	1932
Jack Taylor	Pitcher	1898–1903, 1906–07
Sammy Taylor	Catcher	1958–62
Tony Taylor	Second Base	1958–60
Zack Taylor	Catcher	1929–33
Bud Teachout	Pitcher	1930–31
Patsy Tebeau	First Base	1887
Amaury Telemaco*	Pitcher	1996–98
John Tener	Pitcher	1888–89
Adonis Terry	Pitcher	1894–97
Zeb Terry	Shortstop	1920–22
Wayne Terwilliger	Second Base	1949–51
Bob Tewksbury	Pitcher	1987–88
Moe Thacker	Catcher	1958, 1960–62
Ryan Theriot*	Second Base	2005
Frank Thomas	Outfielder	1960–61, 1966
Lee Thomas	Outfielder	1966–67
Red Thomas	Outfielder	1921
Scot Thompson	Outfielder	1978–83
Bobby Thomson	Outfielder	1958–59
Andre Thornton	Designated Hitter	1973–76
Walter Thornton	Outfielder	1895–98
Bob Thorpe	Pitcher	1955

Dick Tidrow	Pitcher	1979–82
Bobby Tiefenauer	Pitcher	1968
Ozzie Timmons*	Designated Hitter	1995–96
Ben Tincup	Pitcher	1928
Joe Tinker	Shortstop	1902–12, 1916
Bud Tinning	Pitcher	1932–34
Al Todd	Catcher	1940–41, 1943
Jim Todd	Pitcher	1974, 1977
Chick Tolson	First Base	1926–27, 1929–30
Ron Tompkins	Pitcher	1971
Fred Toney	Pitcher	1911–13
Hector Torres	Shortstop	1971
Paul Toth	Pitcher	1962–64
Steve Trachsel*	Pitcher	1993–99
Jim Tracy	Outfielder	1980–81
Bill Traffley	Catcher	1878
Fred Treacey	Outfielder	1874
Bill Tremel	Pitcher	1954–56
Manny Trillo	Second Base	1975–78, 1986–88
Coaker Triplett	Outfielder	1938
Steve Trout	Pitcher	1983–87
Harry Truby	Second Base	1895–96
Michael Tucker*	Outfielder	2001
Pete Turgeon	Shortstop	1923
Ted Turner	Pitcher	1920
Babe Twombly	Outfielder	1920–21
Lefty Tyler	Pitcher	1918–21
Earl Tyree	Catcher	1914
Jim Tyrone	Outfielder	1972, 1974–75
Wayne Tyrone	Outfielder	1976
Mike Tyson	Second Base	1980–81
U		
John Upham	Pitcher	1967–68
Bob Usher	Outfielder	1952
V		
Mike Vail	Outfielder	1978–80
Pedro Valdes*	Left Field	1996, 1998

Ismael Valdez*	Pitcher	2000
Raul Valdez*	Pitcher	2004–05
Vito Valentinetti	Pitcher	1956–57
Jermaine Van Buren*	Pitcher	2005
George Van Haltren	Outfielder	1887–89
Todd Van Poppel	Pitcher	2000–01
Ben Van Ryn	Pitcher	1998
Ike Van Zandt	Outfielder	1904
Hy Vandenberg	Pitcher	1944–45
Johnny Vander Meer	Pitcher	1950
Andy Varga	Pitcher	1950–51
Gary Varsho	Outfielder	1988–90
Carlos Vasquez*	Pitcher	2004–05
Hippo Vaughn	Pitcher	1913–21
Emil Verban	Second Base	1948–50
Dave Veres*	Pitcher	2003
Randy Veres	Pitcher	1994
Joe Vernon	Pitcher	1912
Tom Veryzer	Shortstop	1983–84
Tom Vickery	Pitcher	1891
Hector Villanueva	Catcher	1990–92
Jose Vizcaino*	Shortstop	1991–93
Otto Vogel	Outfielder	1923–24
Bill Voiselle	Pitcher	1950

W

Rube Waddell	Pitcher	1901
Ben Wade	Pitcher	1948
Gale Wade	Outfielder	1955–56
David Wainhouse*	Pitcher	2000, 2001
Eddie Waitkus	First Base	1941, 1946–48
Charlie Waitt	Outfielder	1877
Matt Walbeck	Catcher	1993
Chico Walker	Outfielder	1985–87, 1991–92
Harry Walker	Outfielder	1949
Jack Wallace	Catcher	1915
Mike Walker	Pitcher	1995
Roy Walker	Pitcher	1917
Rube Walker	Catcher	1948–51
Todd Walker*	Second Base	2004–05
Tye Waller	Third Base	1981–82

Joe Wallis	Outfielder	1975–78
Lee Walls	Outfielder	1957–59
Tom Walsh	Catcher	1906
Jerome Walton	Outfielder	1989–92
Chris Ward	Outfielder	1972, 1974
Dick Ward	Pitcher	1934
Preston Ward	First Base	1950, 1953
Lon Warneke	Pitcher	1930–36, 1942, 1943, 1945
Hooks Warner	Third Base	1921
Jack Warner	Pitcher	1962–65
Rabbit Warstler	Shortstop	1940
Carl Warwick	Outfielder	1966
Fred Waterman	Third Base	1875
Scott Watkins	Pitcher	1998–99
Doc Watson	Pitcher	1913
Eddie Watt	Pitcher	1975
David Weathers*	Pitcher	2001
Harry Weaver	Pitcher	1917–19
Jim Weaver	Pitcher	1934
Orlie Weaver	Pitcher	1910–11
Earl Webb	Outfielder	1927–28
Mitch Webster	Outfielder	1988–89
Ray Webster	First Base	1971
Jake Weimer	Pitcher	1903–05
Lefty Weinert	Pitcher	1927–28
Butch Weis	Outfielder	1922–25
Johnny Welch	Pitcher	1926–28, 1931
Todd Wellemeyer*	Pitcher	2003–05
Turk Wendell	Pitcher	1993–97
Don Wengert	Pitcher	1998
Rip Wheeler	Pitcher	1923–24
Pete Whisenant	Outfielder	1956
Deacon White	Third Base	1876
Derrick White*	First Base	1998
Elder White	Shortstop	1962
Jerry White	Outfielder	1978
Rondell White*	Outfielder	2000–01
Warren White	Third Base	1875
Earl Whitehill	Pitcher	1939
Bob Wicker	Pitcher	1903–06

Charlie Wiedemeyer	Pitcher	1934
Milt Wilcox	Pitcher	1975
Hoyt Wilhelm	Pitcher	1970
Harry Wilke	Third Base	1927
Curtis Wilkerson	Shortstop	1989–90
Dean Wilkins	Pitcher	1989–90
Rick Wilkins*	Catcher	1991–95
Bob Will	Outfielder	1957–58, 1960–63
Art Williams	Outfielder	1902
Billy Williams	Outfielder	1959–74
Brian Williams*	Pitcher	2000
Cy Williams	Outfielder	1912–17
Dewey Williams	Catcher	1944–47
Jerome Williams*	Pitcher	2005 (Present)
Mitch Williams	Pitcher	1989–90
Otto Williams	Shortstop	1903–04
Pop Williams	Pitcher	1902–03
Wash Williams	Outfielder	1885
Ned Williamson	Third Base	1879–89
Scott Williamson*	Pitcher	2005 (Present)
Bump Wills	Second Base	1982
Jim Willis	Pitcher	1953–54
Walt Wilmot	Outfielder	1890–95
Art Wilson	Catcher	1916–17
Craig Wilson*	Third Base	2004
Enrique Wilson*	Second Base	2005
Hack Wilson	Outfielder	1926–31
Steve Wilson	Pitcher	1989–91
Willie Wilson	Outfielder	1993–94
Ed Winceniak	Third Base	1956–57
Kettle Wirts	Catcher	1921–23
Casey Wise	Second Base	1957
Harry Wolfe	Shortstop	1917
Harry Wolter	Outfielder	1917
Harry Wolverton	Third Base	1898–00
Tony Womack*	Shortstop	2003
Kerry Wood*	Pitcher	1998, 2000–05
Brad Woodall	Pitcher	1999
Gary Woods	Outfielder	1982–85
Jim Woods	Third Base	1957

Walt Woods	Pitcher	1898
Tim Worrell*	Pitcher	2000
Chuck Wortman	Shortstop	1916–18
Bob Wright	Pitcher	1915
Dave Wright	Pitcher	1897
Mel Wright	Pitcher	1960–61
Pat Wright	Second Base	1890
Rick Wrona	Catcher	1988–90
Michael Wuertz*	Pitcher	2004–05
Marvell Wynne	Outfielder	1989–90
Hank Wyse	Pitcher	1942–47

Y

George Yantz	Catcher	1912
Eric Yelding	Shortstop	1993
Jay Yennaco		2000–01
Carroll Yerkes	Pitcher	1932–33
Steve Yerkes	Second Base	1916
Lefty York	Pitcher	1921
Tony York	Shortstop	1944
Gus Yost	Pitcher	1893
Elmer Yoter	Third Base	1927–28
Anthony Young	Pitcher	1994–95
Danny Young	Pitcher	2000
Don Young	Outfielder	1965, 1969
Eric Young*	Second Base	2000–01

Z

Zip Zabel	Pitcher	1913–15
Geoff Zahn	Pitcher	1975–76
Carlos Zambrano*	Pitcher	2001–05
Eduardo Zambrano	Outfielder	1993–94
Oscar Zamora	Pitcher	1974–76
Rollie Zeider	Second Base	1916–18
Todd Zeile	Third Base	1995
George Zettlein	Pitcher	1874–75
Bob Zick	Pitcher	1954
Don Zimmer	Third Base	1960–61
Heinie Zimmerman	Third Base	1907–16
Julio Zuleta	First Base	2000–01
Dutch Zwilling	Outfielder	1916